LOVE IMPATIENT,
LOVE UNKIND

LOVE IMPATIENT, LOVE UNKIND

EROS HUMAN AND DIVINE

MARK PATRICK HEDERMAN

A Crossroad Book
The Crossroad Publishing Company
New York

The Crossroad Publishing Company
16 Penn Plaza, 481 Eighth Avenue
New York, NY 10001

Library of Congress Cataloging-in-Publication Data
Hederman, Mark Patrick.
      [Manikon eros]
      Love impatient, love unkind : eros human and divine / Mark Patrick Hederman.
          p.   cm.
      Originally published: Manikon eros. Dublin, Ireland : Veritas Publications, 2000.
      Includes bibliographical references.
      ISBN 0-8245-2145-5 (alk. paper)
      1. God – Worship and love.   2. Love – Religious aspects – Christianity.   I. Title.
BV4817.H43 2004
241'.4 – dc22
                                                           2004006966

1   2   3   4   5   6   7   8   9   10   10   09   08   07   06   05   04

This book comes through seven seals,
who know who and where they are.

Whenever the seventh seal is broken,
there is silence in heaven for about half an hour.

CONTENTS

Chapter One

BLOOD ON THE MOON

I WANT TO CATCH YOU at a time, a certain time. You will recognize this time if I describe it properly. If you do not recognize it, then this book is not for you.

The time is one that mostly comes at evening. After a day's work, I stand in the center of my room. I have flicked through the pages of a book looking for something I know I'll never find in books. Outside, there is calm and beauty in a sunset. In the middle distance, too far away to be heard distinctly, is the sound of voices. The sound is the sound of life being lived by someone I do not know. And it brings tears that wither under the heavy knowledge that I have not got it, that I am not really living.

What can I do? I must do something to get away from it, shrug it off. Tomorrow, maybe, it won't be there. Shall I go to bed and turn this time quickly and painlessly into tomorrow? But it will come again. I shall forget about it until it comes. But when it does I shall recognize it. Its empty touch will be familiar. What is this thing? I could give it a name, but it is not that exactly. And, anyway, I would rather you said it for yourself.

I am talking about desire and not about need. I *need* food. When I am physically hungry I eat, and the eating satisfies. Drinking satisfies my thirst. Desire is different: It is never satisfied; it always wants more. The more it gets, the more it wants. Desire is not a need; it is you. It is you when you don't know what you want or what you need, but you do know that you want something, you need something. You have no idea what that something is. Perhaps it isn't a thing at all. You are sad in a way that makes it impossible to do even those things that fill up the day and distract from the ache of something else.

Someone tries to cheer you up. Is there anything in the whole wide world you would like to do? Anywhere you would like to go? And you say either yes or no. The answer doesn't really matter. Even if you do go to that place where you felt happy once, even if you do turn today into tomorrow through a bottle of whiskey or whatever, soon you'll wake up again. And as you wake, you will know that there was something. It will be, at first, not exactly an ache, but the memory of an ache, which will slowly freshen and focus into the familiar pattern. And we know from experience that this vacuum at the base of our consciousness, this empty cave, is the one we have to crawl into, and make sense of, if we are to come to terms with who we really are.

In his novel *A Passage to India*, E. M. Forster uses the Marabar caves as a symbol for this space. The "real

India," toward which the novel tries to forge a passage, is not a geographical place. It is a reality, a place within ourselves, beyond our ordinary everyday experience. The novel fuses the real with the symbol, the personal with the cosmic. The Marabar caves are a framework and a touchstone of Forster's essential quest as a human being. The Marabar caves become an image of the hollowness at the center of each of us. They are the external shape of an inner reality, the landscape of our inscape.

The Marabar caves in themselves are dark and empty spaces within a mountain range, honeycombed by internal bubbles. "The caves are readily described," Forster tells us:

> A tunnel eight feet long, five feet high, three feet wide, leads to a circular chamber about twenty feet in diameter. This arrangement occurs again and again throughout the group of hills, and this is all, this is a Marabar cave. Having seen one such cave, having seen two, having seen three, four, fourteen, twenty-four, the visitor returns to Chandrapore uncertain whether he has had an interesting experience or a dull one or any experience at all.[1]

In fact, the experience to be had in such caves is the experience of nothing.

The purpose of the novel is to describe what happened to one young woman, Adela Quested, when she was brought on a tour of these caves by Aziz, a young

Indian doctor. She entered one of the caves, and something happened to her inside that made her rush out in a frenzy and race down the mountainside, through poisonous brambles and cacti, unaware of the way she was being torn and disfigured by them. Eventually she is discovered in a state of confusion and breakdown by the British governor and his wife, with whom she has been staying.

What accounts for such an experience, such behavior, such an outcome? The only possible explanation is that Adela has been raped by Aziz in the Marabar caves. In the lexicon of most human beings, the only available analogy for otherworldly experience is sexual experience. The court of law investigates the scandal and tries Dr. Aziz for the unpardonable crime of making lewd advances toward a white woman. In the strange anticlimax of the novel, Miss Quested answers that Aziz did not molest her. The prosecuting attorney can hardly believe his ears, can hardly credit such betrayal. His only questions about the Marabar caves are these: "What miscreant lurked in them, presently to be detected by the activities of the law? Who was the guide, and had he been found yet? What was the 'echo' of which the girl complained? He did not know, but presently he would know. Great is information, and she shall prevail."[2]

What is this woman up to? Is she saying that all this rumpus was based on nothing, that nothing happened in the Marabar caves?

This is precisely what the novel is implying, in ways more subtle than the language of law can convey. Nothing happened to Miss Quested in the Marabar caves, and the experience of nothing was so overwhelming that it changed her completely. For this experience, she later wrote to Dr. Aziz, she owed a debt that she could never repay.

The transformation, the transfiguration, that occurred in the Marabar caves was recognized by another character in the novel, Mr. Fielding. It gave him "a new-born respect" for Miss Quested because "although her hard schoolmistressy manner remained, she was no longer examining life, but being examined by it; she had become a real person." Not only did Fielding recognize the change, what the experience in the Marabar cave had wrought in the person and the being of Miss Quested, whom he had, up to that moment, despised; he also recognized ruefully that in his lifetime he had never had such an awakening, that the moment of the Marabar caves had passed him by "with averted face and on swift wings":

> He experienced nothing himself; it was as if someone had told him there was such a moment, and he was obliged to believe. And he felt dubious and discontented suddenly, and wondered whether he was really and truly successful as a human being. After forty years' experience, he had learnt to manage his life and make the best of it on advanced European lines, had developed his

personality, explored his limitations, controlled his passions — and he had done it all without becoming either pedantic or worldly. A creditable achievement, but as the moment passed, he felt he ought to have been working at something else the whole time — he didn't know at what, never would know, never could know, and that was why he felt sad.[3]

It is this desire, this mood, this sadness, that is the subject of my investigation. If you recognize it as yours, then our discussion has begun. This is not an intellectual discourse. This is a dialogue based upon a common experience. My claim is that this mood is shared by all. More than that, I claim that it springs from a zone of our makeup that is fundamental to what we are as human beings. Such moods are ambassadors from the land of our deepest selves. We must take them seriously. They can tell us a great deal about what we really are.

At the deepest level of ourselves we are an emptiness. We are inclined to ride around this vacuum like a crazy biker circles a wall of death. We know that to stop is to fall. The source of our desire is the specter of this nothingness. We want to avoid it, leap out of it into the arms of some other who is not a prey to its corroding pervasiveness. If we learned to accommodate it, however, if we were prepared to let "nothing" happen in our lives, we would slip more comfortably and more appropriately into what we are.

The first thing these moods reveal is that we do not, at all times, fit naturally into the lives we lead. We are by nature misfits. We are not like ants or bees. We do not naturally or instinctually carry on from one end of the day to the other, from one year to the next. There are moments when the mood of restlessness overtakes us and we wonder what it is all about, why we do what we do, why we live the way we live. We are not always completely at ease. Something in our nature is lacking. We feel a void. We cannot say what it is, but we experience it as incompleteness. We are alone and it is not enough.

Before we were born, we lay in the womb in perfect and total luxury. If we live to be a hundred, we shall never experience the complete physical comfort and satisfaction of life in the womb. Here we are surrounded and penetrated by a liquid silk cocoon. In the womb there is no distinction between the world and me, between nature and myself. I and the universe are one. In such perfect unity and harmony there is no such thing as desire. Desire is the gap between what I *am* and what I *want*. In the womb there is no such division. All that I want is immediately supplied without pause or frustration. I do not even notice the distinction between myself and my surroundings. I am are steeped in an unconscious state of passive contentment. A Jewish proverb tells us: "In the mother's body we know the universe. In birth we forget it."

If we were destined for such natural and physical completion, we should never have been born. We were, however, destined for another kind of life. Once we were pushed out into the light and freshness of the world as newborn things, it took us quite some time to realize that this separation had taken place, and even longer to understand what it meant. In the womb we lived under the impression that we were everything. The fact of birth was a catastrophe. When the newborn child stretches out its hand, it does not know that the hand ends with its fingertips. It believes that everything around it is an extension of itself. How could it be otherwise? It is only through painful collision with a world of things that the rude awakening comes: I must end where they begin. Eventually I establish the boundaries of myself, the skin that separates me from all that is not me and prevents me from pouring out to dissolution. I become aware of the slender territory of the "I."

This may sound like an exciting adventure: exploring the island of myself. But to the disinherited divinity it is a shocking disappointment. Without warning or consultation, I find myself stranded on my own in a world that is antipodean to the one I have just left. I am Napoleon exiled on Elba; there is nothing in it for me.

All of a sudden there is a gap between the baby and the world around it. This gap is the birth of desire. And make no mistake about it, this gap is a world-eater: I want everything, not just this or that. I want to return to that state where everything surrounded me closely, permanently, and with warmth.

There is also the exasperating corollary of paralysis, helplessness, impotence. I want all, and can do nothing to achieve this goal. I am so bereft by this *reductio ad absurdum,* I lack even the vocabulary to curse about it. I am unable to know what I want or to articulate it. Least of all can I procure for myself the object of my desire. I want everything and am capable of nothing; that is the definition of humanity.

I therefore express my general state of dissatisfaction and discomfort in an inarticulate roar, which lasts until something is done about it. And this roar, this cry of frustration, follows us all through our lives. It echoes like some sonorous perfume, wafting nausea through all activity, all moments of joy, all times of sorrow, even moments without any special color to mark them off. The ache of desire is one we carry with us always to remind us that there must be something more. That is why it can be called "metaphysical" — it is beyond (*meta*) the physical. We are uncomfortable, abnormal, anomalous misfits; neither fish nor flesh, we are more like centaurs, fauns, or hybrid mongrels, mermaids or flying fish, black swans, white blackbirds, and freaks of nature.

We are not like plants, rooted in "one dear perpetual place" (Yeats), opening themselves naturally to the influence of the sun. Nor are we like insects, totally absorbed in their daily routine. The bee never questions the role of a honey-maker in the modern world. These creatures are naturally connected to their socioeconomic environment. They are at home in the universe.

We are different. As we are carrying the honey to the hive, we can see a bald head below us and think what a change it would be to use the honey as a bomb. We are not "at home" in the world. We are inadequate, ill-equipped, restless. We can try, and many do try, to re-create for ourselves the physical comfort that was ours in the womb — instant feeding, perfect temperature, constant attendance, and permanent security. In our bath, in our beds, in our lavishly furnished apartments, in the arms of a lover, in the euphoria of drugs or the drowsiness of drink, we try to close that gap, to destroy the distance between ourselves and all that is not ourselves. But eventually the bathwater goes cold, and we are left with the inescapable realization that we have to get out, we have to move on. There is nothing we can do about it. We were not built for permanence. We cannot have it all. We are destined for other things. This is why we are beings of desire. The fact of being born into a world for which we are unsuited makes us frustrated creatures; this frustration defines us as metaphysical animals.

Reason is the effect of such tragic circumstances. I think only because I have to. I have no other instrument of pitting my inadequacy against the odds that surround me. Reason is secondary. It helps to describe the way in which I come to terms with my being-in-the-world. This being itself is desire. It is as if I were allergic to the conditions in which I found myself, and the irritation created by my allergy created a boil that eventually burst into a rational brain! Those who claim that this hastily constructed emergency kit is what actually defines us as human beings are not seeing the oyster for the pearl, are mistaking the periscope for the submarine.

Some consider the hypnotism of desire to be a foolish, adolescent thing, the restlessness of spoiled children who have had too much too quickly and don't appreciate what they've got. If you had bone cancer, they say, or if you were crippled or starving, you would soon give up this kind of thing. Or, if you were busy — kicking a football, earning your living — you wouldn't have time for this bubble bath of self-pity. And they are mostly right.

It is true that this is the disease of the well-to-do, those who have got most of what they need. It isn't that we lack anything in particular. We can pinpoint nothing that would respond to this void. It is not a need at all. It is desire. It is also true that if we had to worry about needs — food, life, position, wealth, peace, warmth, health — we would have less time for desire. But having less time does not mean having no desire. All these needs are more or less sophisticated distractions from the real poverty of who we are. When all have been fed, housed, clothed, when the world has become a welfare state and everybody in it is comfortable, it is only then that the real tragedy will become apparent and the real work for humanity will have to begin. Because only then can we accede to the actual reality of who we are. Drudgery, slavery, starvation, and pain can produce some very noble and exceptional people, but they do not, of themselves, make us real human beings.

It is possible to ridicule, shame, or frighten us into ignoring or forgetting this desire. Inexplicable moods, which seep like smoke into even the most successful moments of our lives, can be dissolved and diffused through a carefully programmed life. But such a program cannot extinguish the fire from which the smoke comes, the fire that continues to smolder at the center of ourselves. And the more fire is neglected, the more it belches smoke. We can ignore smoke up to a point, saying that it shouldn't be there, that it's all in our imagination. We can leave the room or spray it with fresheners. But the smoke still exists, and it is not just an unpleasant reality in itself; it's also a signal. It points to the fire. There are three things you can do with fire. You can put it out, you can let it put you out, or you can use it creatively so that it becomes a source of warmth and light.

This mood I have been describing, this smoke, is the perfume of desire, which issues from the depths of our being as men and women. It points to what we are. If we avoid it, flee from it, or are just overcome by it, we never discover what it really is or what we really are.

There are two ways of dealing with desire: kill it or live it, renounce it entirely or seek to coexist with it. There are no half measures. If you allow it to live, it will never be satisfied until it finds what it seeks. Desire roams ceaselessly until it is destroyed by satisfaction or annihilation.

But annihilation is not really possible. Desire is born with my birth. It is my being as a metaphysical animal. It is the void in me that makes me insufficient to myself. We can talk of sacrifice or the renunciation of desire — these concern the things I desire, the objects. Annihilation, however, would require the subject of desire also to be removed. This is why annihilation of desire is impossible. Whatever I may do, or have, or be, at some later time, or in some other dimension, will not be done, had, or lived by me unless I am there to desire it and taste it. Sacrifice of objects of desire — of power, of possession, of life itself — is a possibility, but sacrifice of desire itself is a contradiction, an absurdity. It is not possible to obliterate our identity and remain what we are.

Somehow, we need to live our desire, satisfying, or at least accommodating, our being as desire. One way is to renounce this desire. Renouncing means refusing to satisfy. We contain, we control. We keep ourselves away from whatever might excite our desire. We disconnect.

The other way is fulfillment, which looks for something or someone to fill the void. Though we often regard renunciation and fulfillment as contraries, the difference between these two ways of living desire is not in the desire itself but in the object of that desire. Fulfillment can find its object in more obvious places — sex, fame. . . . The way of waiting or postponing finds its object in less familiar surroundings. It often supposes another world from the one we now inhabit — a different time, a different space, a world beyond, above, or after (maybe eternally ever after) this one. The attainment of such a world is the object of desire for those who have not been deceived by the illusion of this one.

The way of waiting is the eschatological way of fulfilling our desire. God, they tell us, made us to be happy with him forever in heaven. To see whether or not we deserve such happiness, God placed us in an earthly paradise, a sensual minefield, which shall test our true mettle. If we succeed in waiting patiently with eyes closed, curiosity fettered, and desire in check, we shall be rewarded in heaven.

The motivation for living our desire in one way or the other can be religious or fastidious, skeptical or hedonistic. We can decide that this world and what it offers is all that there is and set about conscientiously exploiting that possibility, drinking deeply until the wine runs out. Or turning our eyes to a better world, we can see this one as a trap to seduce us into further misery by whetting our appetite and frustrating its appeasement. So out of desire we resign ourselves to emotionlessness, seeing any movement to quench the thirst as mere aggravation of the appetite without any corresponding satisfaction. Or we can understand pleasure as something to be savored and sipped rather than gulped. Renunciation becomes training in the connoisseurship and expertise that allow us to maximize delight and cultivate orgiastic virtuosity.

Whether we become Circe or Casanova, Marcus Aurelius or Queen Victoria, Madame Bovary or the Marquis de Sade depends upon the attitude we have toward the objects of our desires and the strategy we adopt to diminish or aggrandize them.

What is the object of desire? It is our God. It doesn't really matter what we mean by the word "god." For most people God is equivalent to whatever is going to fulfill. "The secret of our being," says Dostoevsky, "is not only to live, but to have something to live for."

In summary, desire defines us as human beings. It is something that each of us can recognize all too easily as the fundamental flaw lurking in the background of our lives. It is the texture of who we are. Desire is the dimension of space and time. Before it, all was present and all was one. There was no gap between myself and all the rest; there was no past or future in existence. All was totally and eternally present to the unborn I. In birth, the "I" became a being of desire. Between myself and every other stretched a world of space and time. History and geography formed the tissue of such being-in-the-world. Before I was pushed out into them, I floated in a utopia of first-person-singular present tense.

Desire is restlessness or movement of being that is lonely, that finds itself alone. Desire defines me as a fragment cut off and drifting. It is a realization of fragility and impermanence. It is the sadness of change. It seeks rest. It seeks the abolition of space and time.

Chapter Two

THE SOURCE, THE MOVEMENT, AND THE OBJECT OF DESIRE

DESIRE IS THAT WITHIN US which looks for love, which can never be happy or satisfied or at rest until it finds it. Love is union. Union is destruction of my being as lonely, as separated, as restless.

In itself, as itself, desire is movement. Like all movement it goes from one source, one place, toward some other, some object. For the purpose of our investigation, it is therefore possible to divide it into these three elements: source, movement, and object.

The source is the void, the emptiness, the nothing — that barren desert that is me in the company of myself. I am not self-sufficient; I am not total or permanent satisfaction for myself. Two of the most famous documentaries of desire in Western literature are St. Augustine's *Confessions* and Gustave Flaubert's *Madame Bovary*. Augustine's desire tries to find satisfaction in other human beings, but they are found wanting. Addressing God, he writes:

> I long for thee with unquenchable longing. There is sure repose in Thee and life untroubled.... I went away from Thee in my youth and I became to myself a barren land.[1]

He recalls his emotions when his great friend died:

> My heart was black with grief. Whatever I looked upon had the air of death. My native place was a prison-house and my home a strange unhappiness. The things we had done together became sheer torment without him. My eyes were restless looking for him, but he was not there. I hated all places because he was not in them.... I became a great enigma to myself and I was forever asking my soul why it was sad and why it disquieted me so sorely. And my soul knew not what to answer me.... I had no delight but in tears, for tears had taken the place my friend had held in the love of my heart.... I was wretched, and every soul is wretched that is bound in affection of mortal things: it is tormented to lose them, and in their loss becomes aware of the wretchedness which in reality it had even before it lost them.... That first grief had pierced so easily and so deep only because I had spilt out my soul upon the sand, in loving a mortal man as if he were never to die.

The revelation of the source of desire, of the reality of what we are as human beings, comes, according to Augustine, through the experience of love for another human being. This opens up the path and leads us to excavate the depths of our own emptiness. We experience ourselves as a barren desert. This makes us aware of our desire for whatever will fill that void. And so, turning to God he says:

> No man loses Thee, unless he goes from Thee; and in going from Thee, where does he go or where does he flee save from Thee to Thee. . . . Wherever the soul of man turns, unless toward God, it cleaves to sorrow, even though the things outside God and outside itself to which it cleaves may be things of beauty.
>
> Be not foolish, my soul. Listen. The Word Himself calls you to return, and with Him is the place of peace that shall not be broken, where your love will not be forsaken, unless it forsake.

The next extract, from *Madame Bovary,* is also about that desire which is common to us all:

> No matter, she still wasn't happy, she never had been. What caused this inadequacy in her life? Why did everything she leaned on instantaneously decay? . . . Oh, if somewhere there were a being strong and handsome, a valiant heart, passionate and sensitive at once, a poet's spirit in an angel's

form . . . then why should she not find that being?
Vain dream! There was nothing that was worth going far to get: all was lies! Every smile concealed a
yawn of boredom, every joy a misery. Every pleasure brought its surfeit; and the loveliest kisses
only left upon your lips a baffled longing for a more
intense delight. . . .

They knew each other too well to feel that astonishment in possession which multiplies its joy a
hundredfold. She was as sated with him as he was
tired of her. Emma had rediscovered in adultery
all the banality of marriage. . . .

She continued none the less to write him love-
letters, in accordance with the view that a woman
should always write to her lover.

But as she wrote she saw another man, a phan-
tom made of her most ardent memories, of the
finest things she had read, of her most violent
longings; who became in the end so real and so
accessible that he set her thrilling with wonder,
though she had no clear picture of him, for he
receded like a god behind the abundance of his
attributes.[2]

And in the disappointment of purely human love, Emma
Bovary also turns toward God:

Emma felt a powerful influence sweep over her,
relieving her of all pain, all perception, all feeling.
Her flesh found rest from thought; a new life had

begun; it was as if her soul, ascending to God, were about to be swallowed up in His love like burning incense vanishing in smoke.... Then she let her head drop back on to the pillow, seeming to hear through space the harps of the seraphs playing, and to see, seated upon a throne of gold in an azure Heaven with his Saints around Him bearing branches of green palm, God the Father, resplendent in majesty, at whose command angels with wings of flame descended to earth to carry her up in their arms.

This glorious vision remained in her memory as the most beautiful dream that could be dreamed. She strove to recapture the sensation of it, which lingered, if with a less exclusive purity, yet with as profound an enchantment. Her soul, deformed by pride, found rest in Christian humility. Relishing the pleasure of weakness, Emma contemplated the destruction of her will within her, which was to leave the way wide open to the flowing tide of grace. So then, in place of happiness there existed greater felicities, above all loves a higher love, without end or intermission, a love that would grow to all eternity. Amid the illusions that her wishes prompted, she glimpsed a realm of purity, floating above the earth, melting into the sky, where she aspired to be. She wanted to become a saint.[3]

Both these authors describe the source of desire in the same way. It begins in the desert of the heart, where nothing grows and all is impotent. The desolation of this empty place is what makes every man and woman move toward some other to find completion and fulfillment. Both the erotic and the mystical passions, says Denis de Rougemont, "speak one same language, whether because either is cause or effect of the other or because they have a common origin."[4]

So the second element in desire is this movement, the way in which the source reaches out toward an object. It is a movement of desperate possessiveness. We are possessed by the desire for possession. We want to secure for ourselves absolute and total, permanent and unending control over whatever it is that will make us happy.

Shakespeare describes this movement of desire in *Twelfth Night,* the theme of which is love. "If music be the food of love, play on." This is love as "fancy" or infatuation. The scene is set on the island of Illyria (a name that suggests a mixture of hysteria and illusion), to which all are drawn by a magic spell: "A witchcraft drew me hither," Antonio tells us. And each scene and every character is a fantastic unfolding of its many shapes and forms: "So full of shapes is fancy / That it alone is high fantastical." Love is the source of every action, every plot, every joke on this island and in this play. The Duke is in love with Olivia; Olivia is in love with Viola, who, in turn, is in love with the Duke; Antonio is in love with Sebastian; Sebastian falls in love with Olivia; the Duke falls in love with Viola; and the foolish among us might think of this as a happy ending. Except that the Fool, himself the most important mouthpiece for Shakespeare, ends it for us:

> When that I was and a little tiny boy,
> With hey-ho, the wind and the rain;
> A foolish thing was but a toy...

This state of being produces a form of madness that is the same for all those who fall victim to it, whether man or woman, duke or jester. Social or sexual categories are irrelevant. On this island of infatuation, no one knows any kind of reality, either their own or anyone else's. We are dealing with people who are incapable of breaking out of their own imprisonment. The object of their "love" is always an invention of their "fancy," and therefore it has no real identity or form of its own. They are victims of their own particular kind of blindsight. They are in love with love, and "the whirligig of time brings in his revenges." But, in Shakespeare's presentation, this is a purification that can lead to some kind of real love.

For the infatuated ones, however, the object/person who happens to spark off this crazy state of obsession is a mere commodity, an occasion that has no reality in himself or herself. Thus the Duke can switch his infatuation from Olivia to Viola, and Olivia can substitute Sebastian for Viola, without seeming to change the intensity or the feeling. All that matters is that "I shall have a share in

this most happy wrack." It is a dance that needs a partner. The partner chosen to accompany us in this agony
must be divine. "Here comes the countess, now heaven
walks on earth."

Thomas Mann, in the twentieth century, describes exactly the same kind of infatuation in many of his novels.
Here is one example from *Joseph and His Brothers:*

> Oh, muddled fantastic logic of love! So familiar, it
> is hardly worth telling; so old that it . . . seems new
> only to those who . . . are in the throes of what they
> believe to be a unique experience. . . .
>
> A being whom we bless for the tortures he in-
> flicts must be a god, not a man, else we should
> curse him. A certain logicality cannot be denied.
> A being upon whom depends all the joy and sor-
> row of our days — for that is love — belongs in the
> ranks of the divine.[5]

As well as the divinization of the object of love, there is
a corresponding impatience with all time and all space
that separates from constant presence of the beloved.
Shakespeare again:

> Come hither, boy. If ever thou shalt love,
> In the sweet pangs of it, remember me.
> For such as I am all true lovers are:
> Unstaid and skittish in all motions else,
> Save in the constant image of the creature
> That is beloved.[6]

The magic spell of infatuation is a trick of fancy that makes the subject sick with love:

> She pined in thought,
> And with a green and yellow melancholy,
> She sat like Patience on a monument,
> Smiling at grief.[7]

This disease of infatuation turns the world into a nightmare of slavery to one's idol. Thomas Mann gives one of the most accurate descriptions of its contorted movement:

> In love there is a painful, involved, and bewildering struggle; it splits the soul with half-wishing, half-unwishing, so that the lover curses the must-see with as good will as he would blissfully welcome the may-see. And the more violent his anguish from the last time of seeing, the more passionately he strives for the next opportunity to aggravate his disease. This most of all when the patient had ground to rejoice that the pain was growing less! For it can actually happen that a meeting can tarnish the brilliance of the desired object and bring about a certain disappointment, cooling, and detachment.[8]

The paradox of infatuation is that its victim becomes slave to the very object that is sole perpetrator of all this most agonizing torture and misery. All we need to do to dispel the pain is remove ourselves from the other's presence, or have the other removed from ours. It would be as simple as that.

> Such might be the result were one lord and master of one's passion instead of its victim; for the chances of winning the other are greatly improved by the cooling of one's own feelings. But the lover will listen to nothing of all this; the advantages of returning sanity, coolness, and boldness . . . reckons as nothing compared with the loss he imagines that he will suffer by the diminution of his feelings. He declines upon a state of desolation and emptiness comparable to that of a drug-taker deprived of his drug, and strains every muscle to regain his former state of infatuation by fresh doses of re-infecting impressions.
>
> Thus it is with must and may in the field of love's folly. . . . For he, however much he may groan under the lash of his passion, is not only incapable of wishing to be free, he is even incapable of wanting to wish it. He probably knows that if he did not see the object of his passion for a certain time — quite an absurdly short time — he would be free. But it is just forgetting of which he is more afraid than of anything else; indeed, every pain at parting rests upon a secret dread of the inevitable forgetting.[9]

The object of desire, the third element in this analysis, what is desirable, is something perceived as permanent and total, something that will relax me and tranquilize me into forgetting forever the gap that separates me from all that is not myself. Here is Alexander Solzhenitsyn in *The First Circle*, for example, describing one prisoner in a concentration camp: "For the present she wanted to shut everything out of her mind except Gleb. She would think of that timeless entity which was made up not just of him and of her, but of the two of them together, and which we usually call by that overworked word 'love.' "[10]

The object of our love is always a distortion. It is a mixture of reality and fantasy. There are those who would suggest that an embarrassingly large proportion of it is fantasy. We take a perfectly ordinary man or woman and project onto them all our accumulated expectations of an ideal partner. Our imagination turns the pumpkin into the elegant coach and horses. We reinvent the person we have chosen. Psychoanalysis has shown that we carry from our earliest childhood a complete template of the person or thing we are supposedly searching for all our lives. We are hardwired for love, and a largely unconscious lock-on takes place between us and the object of our desire. Whatever part, even bodily part, or characteristic excites our fetishistic obsession becomes the trigger for our automatic spray-gun, which then paints the other whichever way we want that person to look.

Thus Lacan has famously stated that even though we can be enthralled by sexual desire, there is no such thing as a sexual relationship, because our libidinal mechanisms are not involved with another person as such. So as lovers we are like ships passing each other in the night. Or, rather, submarines. We are submerged in a solipsistic psychic miasma, and the periscope, which is just about able to pierce through, has distorted and restricted vision.

The depressing suggestion of Lacan and others seems to be that we never have access to others as they are. We are irretrievably ensconced in our own private world, and "the Real" as such is a transcendent goal, beyond our subjective grasp. Our access to the Real is forever blocked because our camera lens is always focused on "the Thing" that is our substitute fetish, our worry-bead replacement, for reality. The Real, for Lacan, is the symbolic Other, the Not-I — whatever is beyond myself and the world of me. I can never, therefore, actually get into contact with this. It always remains outside my grasp; it always eludes me. I have a whole system inside myself however, that is determined to grasp this Real and tries to identify it with certain privileged objects that turn me on. These become the focus of my desire to know the Real, and my system works overtime plastering imaginative identification tags onto such objects. I confuse them with the Real and therefore can't go any further than myself or have any real external contact.

I am presenting Lacan's view in a highly simplified form, an but even more subtle and comprehensive presentation of it would not undermine or discount what I am saying here about the object of desire.[11] Whether that

object is a real person or a mirage, partly or totally constructed from the psyche of the infatuated subject, does
not matter much. It is still the same object of desire,
whether it is a reality or a fiction. Whatever the difficulties, whatever the obstacles thrown up by our psyche,
we are still relational beings, and our privilege and task
is to reach out and relate to others in a movement of
love, in a particular understanding of this word we will
articulate carefully in later chapters.

In the context of this chapter, however, "love" is the
fulfillment of desire. It is a reality that cannot be known
beforehand; it has to be experienced. When it happens
you know it, you recognize it, and you name it as that
"something" you had always been looking for. Although
it is unique and reinvented in every instance, there is still
something about it that is recognizably the same. Romeo
and Juliet, Tristan and Isolde, Diarmuid and Gráinne,
Antony and Cleopatra, and now you and I, each and all
of us, experience the same fullness. And yet it is always
different for each of us. What happens is the same in
every case. Love is eternally the same. It is always fullness, always satisfaction of desire. Whether it is proven at
a later stage that love in this sense of the word is a thirty-
month whirlwind of infatuation or an illness comparable
to an obsessive compulsive disorder, as some would hold,
is another matter. The fact still persists that such a reality invades our lives and is one of the ways of dealing
with desire.

Impelled by desire we want to destroy a desire within ourselves. To do so means being possessed by that timelessness, spacelessness, forgetfulness that is the permanent and total satisfaction of our desire. This is the magic potion we call love.

Chapter Three

PLEASURE
FOR PLEASURE

A RISTOTLE SAYS OF DESIRE that its nature is to be
without limits. He also suggests that most of our
lives are no more than attempts to satisfy this infinite
lack. It is difficult to stress sufficiently the infinite character of desire. Desire, as my being, wants everything,
always. Its object is as infinite as it is undefined. It seeks
a permanent and total presence. This state we call happiness. Our being is to search for happiness, a maxim
accepted by many philosophers. It was, perhaps, most
compellingly articulated by St. Augustine both in his life
and in his work: "We all want to live happily; in the
whole human race there is no one who does not assent
to this proposition, even before it is fully articulated."[1]
Nothing can end this search except the perfect and enduring realization of this end. Happiness is, therefore,
the ultimate object of desire.

We began by saying that desire was being. As such,
we claimed that it was impossible to annihilate desire
without annihilating ourselves. We then proceeded to

describe satisfaction as the fulfillment of desire through an appropriate object. Is this not a contradiction? Satisfaction (in Latin *satis* = enough + *facere* = to do or to make) means providing ourselves with "enough." If we fill ourselves up as often as we can, this creates a momentary illusion of bliss. A life of bliss then becomes a punctuated series of limited installments of eternal happiness. We settle for a life in which we substitute pleasure for happiness, each time thinking that it is the real thing, but each time having to kill the idol that has proved to be an imposter. Progress is movement from mirage to mirage. So isn't it a contradiction to speak of "satisfaction" at all? The answer is yes, it is a contradiction. But it is *the* contradiction that makes up the nature of desire.

Here it is necessary to introduce another important term. The key to this apparent paradox is to be found in the notion (rather, the reality) of pleasure. Pleasure is what occurs to us most readily and spontaneously as that which will satisfy desire.

And you must know what I am talking about when I speak of pleasure. Pleasure is not pleasure if it leaves any part of me outside it. If I am conscious of it, or absent from it, in any way, it ceases to be pleasure. If I am watching myself enjoying myself, then I am actually engaged in neither activity. Pleasure must be an actual moment that makes a complete whole out of the elements it comprises. *Delectatio*, the sages of the old world would repeat, *tota et simul*. Pleasure is a simultaneity. I can look back on it, I can look forward to it, but while it is on, I must be absorbed by it. If I am not, then it ceases to be. Pleasure is not pleasure if it allows even a whisper of self-consciousness. It collects everything into its present moment, exhausting both me and itself in an ecstasy, making time and myself stand still. Aristotle called it an indivisible whole.

Pleasure is instant eternity. While it lasts it is perfect and replete. The fact that it is limited and finite must not blind us to its seamless quality as a moment in itself. The limitation does not invade the pleasure, which is oblivious to it. In itself, as itself, pleasure is perfect. This is what we mean by that "timeless entity" that is capable of quenching desire.

At that moment of meeting, when someone is really present, time disappears. The room also disappears. There is no chair, no table, no light, no window. I am not worried about the pimple on my nose, about whether or not I smell, about what the other person thinks of me. On other occasions I am awkward and dispersed. My hands are too big. I am not sure whether to remain standing or to sit. Does she want me to go? Am I taking up his time? Does she see that I am trying to impress her? Or it is the other way around: I am conscious that he is awkward, nervous, fearful, ashamed.

In the moment of real union, of perfect meeting, I am totally present and so is the other person. We are both bound together in this real presence that seems to absorb into itself all space and time. Then someone else comes into the room. The chair returns under me, the table comes to land, the window falls into place, and here am I, and there is the other, and we are being approached by the third who has disturbed the perfection of our communion. We have returned to the state of separation, to the land of desire. Such is the ambiguity of pleasure and the reason why it can be confused with happiness. There is a contradiction between the finite, limited nature of pleasure and the infinite, limitless nature of happiness. Pleasure thus becomes the rival, even the enemy, of happiness.

Pleasure is perfect and totalizing; it exhausts me in the moment of its actuality. It is exactly what desire would like to be able to achieve in terms of the indefinable happiness it seeks. But it is also what desire will never be able to achieve because desire is infinite and limitless.

This does not prevent us from taking the false currency of pleasure as counterfeit coin to satisfy the immediate craving of desire. We try to make pleasure an absolute. We try to turn the objects around us into idols. Such an attempt belongs also to the nature of desire. For desire, as well as being unquenchable longing, is also the conviction that somewhere over, or under, the rainbow, an object worthy of that longing must exist. Which brings us once again to the paradoxical nature of love.

The being of desire is incapable of annihilation in either the subject or the object of desire. We find ourselves incomplete. This incompleteness is the source of our search for wholeness or fulfillment. Armed with an infinite desire, we find ourselves in a world of finite objects. Although our desire is geared to happiness that only an eternal object can provide, it can focus itself on a finite object and invest this with all the properties of the God for whom we wait. The moment of love, the moment of pleasure, are temporary fulfillment of everlasting hope for what is everlasting. We can live it for the moment and spend our lives swinging from one timeless ecstasy to the next, like a bee moving from flower to flower, sucking the nectar from each, but fully aware that no one flower can ever provide that flow of honey, that ocean of timeless presence, which alone is worthy of the title "happiness" and which alone can fulfill our desire.

This is our situation: the tragic impossibility of destroying desire. Our lives are mostly a search for such destruction. We seek to destroy the fretful movement by combining the source and the goal, by bridging the gap, absorbing one into the other. Such is the impossibility. But this impossibility, which is the reality of desire, is the impossibility we are required to live. It is what we are.

There are three elements we have to include in our attempt to solve the mystery of desire: desire itself, the finite objects of desire (which are the targets of pleasure), and the infinite object of that desire (which we are calling happiness). If we fail to do justice to any of these three aspects of the problem, we are avoiding the issue and failing to come to terms with the reality of our nature.

Thomas Aquinas, whose philosophy has molded much of Western European thinking on all such matters, was quite aware of the three. He describes them as levels of the soul — the vegetal, the sensory, and the spiritual. For Aquinas, each level has its own particular object, which both specifies and defines it. In his thinking, there would be no necessity to divide into such levels if there was no particular object toward which each was geared. Objects mark off one function from another and define each as something in its own right.

We have needs, which we treat as such at a biological level. This level of our being has specific commodities adapted to it. At the other end of the spectrum we have spiritual needs. Aquinas saw, as other thinkers did not, that there is an intermediary level, the psychic, which also has its corresponding wish list, and which makes up a very definite and controversial aspect of our life. The specific object of the psychic or sensory level of our soul is, according to Aquinas, pleasure.

The difficulty is that, despite the three levels and the three objects, there are only two kinds of movement in us to cater to all three realities — the movement of *need* and the movement of *desire.* Desire relates to both the psychic and the spiritual. It relates to the first as finite and to the second as infinite. It cannot relate to both successfully in the same way. Need works at a dual level at the other end of the scale, at the biological and psychic levels. Thus we have three objects and two movements. Three into two won't go.

The answers of moral philosophers and theologians in the past have been strikingly similar. Such answers are important because they form a large part of our cultural heritage and the received wisdom that establishes behavioral patterns and inspires the "natural" reaction to this problem. We are inclined to identify these reactions as "instinctive," which they are not. They are inculcated reactions for the most part, designed to eliminate the object of the second level, in other words, to eliminate pleasure. Pleasure, as such, was refused a valid existence in its own right. Seeing that pleasure can and does substitute itself for the spiritual object of desire, that it can become an idol, usurping the throne of absolute values, the tendency was to cut it out altogether, to deny its existence. The danger of declaring it to be everything caused the pendulum to swing in the opposite direction: It was declared to be nothing.

In the realm of food, a certain amount of pleasurable activity was sanctioned because it was necessary for survival. In other words, it received its justification and its identification from the biological level of existence. Indirectly, it also received sanction from the spiritual level: Without sustenance we cannot pray. But it was never admitted that eating, in itself, was pleasurable and that food, as opposed to nourishment, is the object of a specific and essential level of our being, which is neither biological nor spiritual. Food is meant to be enjoyed as food.

In the case of drink the ambiguity becomes even more transparent. Drinking a bottle of Châteauneuf-du-Pape may be necessary for survival and could, in a pinch, be accounted spiritual homage to the pope on the label, but it is more, and other, than either of these alibis. It constitutes a real and irreducible pleasure in itself.

Some of us will remember grandparents who tottered nightly to bed with great tankards of alcohol, protesting that the vile liquid was for "medicinal purposes." They were under doctor's orders, and otherwise they wouldn't be seen dead imbibing such wickedness — in other words a biological alibi for a pleasurable tipple.

The same stranglehold presided over debates about censorship and pornography in the twentieth century. If the "filth" was there for "spiritual" reasons, it could be justified as "artistic." When director Roman Polanski made a controversial film loosely based upon Shakespeare's *Macbeth,* he had a teenage Lady Macbeth sleepwalk in the nude. The censors discussed the merits of the film and sought some artistic or scientific reasons for legitimizing the otherwise "pornographic" scene. Polanski himself insisted that, although it was indeed historically true that nighties were not worn in sixteenth-century Scotland, his real reason for showing her young and naked was because people would get pleasure from seeing her that way.

We find ourselves talking about "legitimate" pleasures. These are always taken or performed for some other, more noble, reason than the simple pleasure in and for itself. Good for the health, good for the soul. How often we take pleasure in the guise of "charity." We even try to take the "good" out of what others do, denouncing it as "mere pleasure": "She loves doing that. She can't help it, in fact. She'd be miserable without her poor."

The problem hits the headlines when it enters the domain of sexuality. Sexuality is the domain of pleasure par excellence, where the struggle between pleasure and happiness is likely to become most confused. Here desire is most prone to make an idol of a finite object.

And the question is this: Can I have sexual pleasure for its own sake, without having to justify it with some biological or spiritual support system? A long tradition in such matters would regard sexuality, especially in its genital expression, as a necessary evil. Its purpose is purely biological — the reproduction of the species. Any prolongation of the act, any indulgence in the incidental thrills that accrue, are abuses. Which again suggests that pleasure for its own sake is not a legitimate pursuit.

Whatever solution we adopt to the problem of desire must articulate the appropriate relationship between desire and its ultimate object, which we have called happiness, and its immediate object, which we have identified as pleasure.

Desire is a relation. Like every other relation, this relation has a source, a movement, and an end. It always involves at least two distinguishable realities with some difference or distance between them. We have seen how desire as a source remains constant and indestructible, even though its objects and movements can vary. As well as the ever-present source of desire, we have been able to identify at least two such objects. Both are irreducible to the other; neither can be obliterated. The nature and movement of desire itself must change or be changed to adapt to the object concerned. We cannot short-circuit the discussion by eliminating one of these elements. Nor can we make a finite object into an infinite one. Just as we cannot switch from idols to God in the same movement without involving ourselves in sterile blasphemy, we cannot on the other hand deny the existence of pleasure or the objects of pleasure without indulging in another form of blasphemy. Pleasure may not be everything, but it is something. It is important to establish the nature of that something.

One thing remains constant — the source of desire within ourselves, its being as our being. Whatever way we choose to live this reality, whichever one of the many paths we may follow, this desire is our energetic impetus. Whether we fix our sights on absent or eternal goals, or settle for the more humble realities around us, our inspiration remains the same — that desire which is common to us all and identified with the deepest reality of who we are. Our genius is to become who we are. This means coming to terms with that most basic reality — desire.

We have to keep four pieces of a jigsaw puzzle in play when trying to insert the centerpiece. Each one must be grafted into the piece in the middle, which will complete the picture and soften the edges of all four. This implies a sensitive and versatile hub that will give appropriate and untrammeled action and scope to the source, the movement, and the finite and infinite objects of desire.

Where does such a virtuoso centerpiece come from? Is it an imported extra? Are all four elements transformed by being assumed into a mightier whole, which would submerge their family quarrel into something greater?

Any transformation of desire has to come from me. The transformation may be triggered by some revelation from elsewhere that provides me with the incentive or the wherewithal to change, but the actual change itself cannot be caused without me, or in spite of me.

When I say, therefore, that "love" is the ultimate and perfect "form" of desire, I do not mean that love is something other than desire, an exterior corset, for example, that we put on ourselves to give it shape. Love is a way of living desire. It becomes one with desire.

In all that has been said so far about desire, everything has circulated around me as the subject of desire. Although I began by describing it as a movement toward something other or beyond myself, I still examined this movement through what it sought and could achieve *for me*. The object of desire was also perceived in its potential usefulness to me. It was called pleasure when it produced limited satisfaction; it was called happiness when it achieved ultimate satisfaction. Both these terms described me more than they did any particular object. I planned my campaign of satisfying desire in view of the possibility of possessing these objects. If achievable, I would fire ahead; if not, I would wait. All the discussion centered on desire as having. Its object was a treasure that I could or could not possess.

Such an examination of desire as having, or not having, is a point of view. It is a "natural" point of view for those who are stuck in the cul-de-sac of desire. Our situation is tragic. We do not just know this — we feel it. Every instinct in us struggles against such a death sentence. In the narrow enclosure of our prison we think only of getting out. Like those in concentration camps, we think only of escape. Can I use it, can I use them, as escape routes from this life of solitary confinement? We do not accept that this was the way we were made, or that this was the life we were destined to lead. No one sees the concentration camp as a good career move. We interpret our caged-in frustration as a sign that things were never meant to be like this. We refuse the possibility that this is us as we should be.

This insistence upon presenting desire at the level of having is avoidance of desire at the level of being. We refuse, naturally, to accept that we are desire, that this desire that goads us to reject and escape it is the very texture of who we are. We refuse to lie down in this foul place. We insist that our being was destined for higher, more pleasant things — objects procurable from outside ourselves. These outside objects that are there to be "had" can tear down our prison walls and remove us from this dungeon of ourselves.

It is also clear that the essence of desire is to be. In having, desire ceases to be. This is, again, why we refuse to examine it at any level other than that of having: because we must get rid of it at all costs. We must destroy this reality. If this means the destruction of ourselves, then such would be preferable to accepting that we are, and cannot *not* be, creatures of desire.

All we have been saying about desire in terms of pleasure and happiness has been no more than a rejection of desire as the reality of our being. We have immediately and without reflection run away from the possibility that desire is an inescapable condition of humanity and have set out instead in search of the elixir that would cure us forever of this unnatural disease. We refuse to accept that our condition is incurable. Like invalids cushioned from their illness by a conspiracy of silence or small talk, we will not be told — we refuse to hear — that this is the way things are. Desire as having is built upon the rejection of desire as being. It is a position I adopt, an interpretation of my being, a rejection of myself as I really am.

To understand desire as it really is requires us to allow it to inform us. We must allow it to be. Such acceptance of reality is love. Love is the way we *are* in ourselves and amid the others who surround us. Love is our being-in-the-world as it is and as it should be. We can describe this attitude as "interest" in the original meaning of the word. *Esse* is the Latin word for being, the infinitive "to be"; *inter* means between. The combination of the two spells out a way of being among other realities, my own included. Love is what makes my interest realistic and proportionate. It means that I no longer define everything in terms of *my* desire.

Desire as we have been describing it is a position that I hold, a central place from which I move to conquer and monopolize the world around me. I measure everything according to its value for me. All is weighed up as food, as pleasure, as happiness. Reality is measured in its distance from, and importance to, me. Love, on the other hand, is a dis-position that allows reality to inform me of its real presence.

Let me say it quite simply. One day you discover that an apple, any apple, is not just something to eat. An apple is protective covering for its own seed. When I eat, I destroy rather than fulfill its being as apple. That comes as a surprise.

The transformation of desire into love is not just confusing; it is unidentifiable. We cannot say when or how such transformation occurs. It is not necessary or organic growth from one to the other. Love of myself as I am is not a necessary corollary to being. It is not enough simply to be. I have to choose to be in a certain way. To live is not the same as to love my being. I need never accede to this second dimension. There are some who would claim that love of one's being is tantamount to surrender. Passive acceptance of what one is implies that what I am merits obedience and delight. Many would see this as naivety or optimism. The braver course is to reject that being and force myself into an alternative mold.

It is difficult — at times impossible — to fall out of love as we perceive it from a possessive perspective. We love someone we know we can never have. We feel the cruelty of the situation and no one is to blame. And yet the spell is cast. We cannot give up. We continue to love what we can never have. We reject everything else — all that we have and are. We refuse to *be* unless we can *have* this one person who seems to hold out the possibility of happiness. How do we break the spell? We hear lectures, sermons, logic from our friends. These only help keep us in thrall by their indirect reference to that which is holding us prisoner. They say that time cures all. Does it? And if it does, what does it do?

Desire is such a spell. It is a magic that we have to counter-charm if we do not wish to remain forever in its enchanted forest. Most of us do prefer to remain there. We prefer the pains of servitude to the fresh open space of freedom. Most prefer not to be cured of unrequited love. We pretend that it is a torture from which we beg release. But more than anything else, we fear release, the footloose insignificance of not being hooked to someone else. We dread the plainness of being who we are, the banality of love as it is.

The red and yellow glare of infatuation has a sickly weight that makes it recognizable as emotion. Without it there might be the unbearable lightness of being (Milan Kundera). To us who cannot believe in the true worth of our own being, the thralldom of desire is tangible evidence of our vitality. We hang on and wallow in it in spite of our protests. Until we really want to do so, we find it impossible to undertake another kind of loving.

Thomas Aquinas has this to say of love:

> There are two kinds of love: one is imperfect, the other perfect. Imperfect love is loving something not because it is good in itself, but because it is somehow good for me. This kind of love we call concupiscence, as when we say we love wine for its sweetness, or other persons for their usefulness to us, or the pleasure they afford us.
>
> Perfect love is where we love something for the good that it is in itself; where, for instance, I love someone by wishing that person all the good I can wish, even if none of this should ever accrue to me. This perfect love we call friendship, where someone is loved in and for himself or herself.[2]

If we apply Aquinas's analysis to our own, he seems to be saying that the transformation of desire into love requires the object, which is always "the good" in some shape or form, to be approached not as something good for me, but as something good in itself.

If we read what he says in its proper context, stressing the verb "to be" rather than the notion of "the good," thereby emphasizing the ontological rather than the ethical perspective, it boils down to moving the level of desire from the order of having to the order of being.

I do not search for objects because they are useful to, or pleasurable for, me; instead I make myself present (as I am, in my being) to certain objects that are good in themselves. I make myself really present to what is, as it is, in itself. I love others as they are, for what they are.

Love is presence *to* something, rather than presence *of* something, or someone. It requires of me a certain "object-ivity." This objectivity is, first of all, the capacity to understand what is — the power to know, to understand (in a specific sense) "being" as such, both in myself and in every other reality in the world of things. This kind of knowledge has been called metaphysics. It is a big word but it is an infinitely practical knowledge. It helps us to become objective, because it strips subjectivity and exposes the counterfeit pretender we have inserted.

Such objectivity is the result of a kind of recollection through which we can become present to ourselves. It is a capacity to understand the connection between *(inter-esse)* our being and other beings in the web of reality around us. To connect with all things at the level of their being is to establish our real interest in them. The purpose of such objectivity is to situate and understand this interest of ours. A substitute interest at the level of having is fraudulent, however pleasurable or plausible it appears.

I must no longer see myself as the center or focal point around which everything and everyone else is orchestrated in a field of possible possessions. Instead, I must attempt to establish my own position among things. I must swap my natural physical place for my more real and metaphysical one. We already described the natural, physical relationship of ourselves to our world as an unsatisfactory replacement of the situation in the womb. Time has been given us to exchange this natural, physical relation for a spiritual one. This spiritual relationship is love, in its genuine rather than its counterfeit form. We are given time to become lovers, time to become truly human.

Becoming human is a process of rebirth. Not the birth of flesh and blood, which caused us so much pain and defined our limitations as individual men and women, but rebirth in the spirit of love, which opens out, even within our limitations, infinite horizons that are available to us as lovers. This is the birth of a new world, a world in which we are a part, and not even a central part, in a whole tapestry of being. In the *Tempest* Shakespeare has Miranda (whose name means "wonder") say, after waking up to this mystery: "How beauteous mankind is. / O brave new world, that has such people in't."

Such rebirth in a brave new world is accomplished by a certain kind of knowledge, knowledge of being, which is an act of conceiving both myself and everything that is. Unless my old self dies, it remains alone. It is a lonely measuring substance that takes itself to be the foundation of the only world that really matters. From such a position I am the creator of my own world.

Our perfection as human beings is not in the possession of a thing or an object; nor is it in complete dispossession of ourselves, some kind of emptiness. It is an act — an act of relationship with what really is. It is an act of love. This act is, in itself, renunciation. It is renunciation of all that I am not, and of all that the object is not, in order to concentrate on what I am and on what the object is. It is an act or movement of presence — the real presence of myself, as I am, to whatever *is* before me.

This calls for a continuous awareness that floats like a cork on the waves of desire. It provides balance, which allows assimilation of our growth. It is the constant vigilance over our being and the being of all that comes to meet us. It is the development of our difference. We renounce all that is not us and concentrate on developing the reality of who we really are.

In the same movement whereby we develop the specific reality of ourselves, we establish and identify the otherness of the other. Our life, our desire, assumes its responsibility only when it becomes such service of what really is. This is renunciation as life itself — letting the flowers grow, recognizing that each person's genius is to be himself or herself.

Renunciation is not a lonely self-discipline that I cultivate within myself as a virtuous program before embarking upon the life of desire. It does not come before desire as a preliminary. Nor does it come after desire as a remorseful decision to keep myself in check. Renunciation must be the interior structure of desire itself. As such, it is an act of relation that is the paradoxical confirmation of both the object and the subject of desire. No previous preparation or subsequent remorse can help me live the actual relation. Relation can be perfected only as relation. Renunciation, as the realization of the reciprocal difference between me as subject and the other as object, must be accomplished by and through the act of relating itself. The relationship is the place where the learning, the understanding, the perfecting take place. Relationship teaches me to be me, and you to be you; it shows us, as no other exercise can, how to love me as me, you as you, and to love the ineradicable differences between us.

Renunciation is the act of love. It is the act of being precisely who I am and affording you that same privilege. In the presence of finite objects that have become for us absolute idols, we strain to prove the authenticity of our love, justifying its exclusivity by the intensity of our commitment. We exaggerate. We invest this obsessional object with an overdose of being, which deprives the rest of the world, including ourselves, of their proportionate share.

Love is the power to be and to let be. To live it chastely is to wield it effectively. Chastity is the appropriate language of desire. It respects and loves the difference between, and it honors and acknowledges the integrity and impenetrability of each and every other. Chastity is renunciation within the act of love. It is what allows the ecstasy of orgasm, for instance, to be entirely personal as well as self-transcending.

Chapter Four

THIRSTING
FOR GOD

L ET US NOW EXAMINE the theology of desire — the
application of this faculty in its source, its movement, and its object or end, as we have described these,
to what we call God. Is it true that only God is adequate
to our desire, that, as St. Augustine says: "Our hearts
are restless till they rest in Thee"? If it is true, then is
it sufficient to change the object while maintaining both
the movement and the source of our desire? If there is
such an object as God, then is the natural movement
of our desire sufficient to reach him, or must there be
some transformation of the essence of desire to make it
adequate to this newfound goal?

Does this desire for God spell sheer frustration? Does
it mean that we couldn't find anything else, that all
else proved deficient? Does it mean that we were clever
enough to spot the decoy and so turn our attention to
the one thing that mattered, that we learned young and
early to expect nothing but frustration from this world
and focused our desire on something more worthwhile?

Does it mean that the source and movement of desire remain as we have described them, barren and possessive, and that these are then applied, without change or transformation, to a bigger, better, and more worthy object? Does it mean that we become theosexual — that what a human lover is for other people, God becomes for us?

Is it possible and is it right to use God as the ultimate quencher of desire? There is a long and venerable tradition of religious thinkers who not only find it right and fitting, but who see desire as a trick used by God to draw us toward him. George Herbert puts it poetically:

THE PULLEY

When God at first made man,
Having a glasse of blessings standing by,
"Let us," said He, "poure on him all we can;
Let the world's riches, which dispersèd lie,
  Contract into a span."

So strength first made a way;
Then beautie flow'd, then wisdome, honour, pleasure;
When almost all was out, God made a stay,
Perceiving that, alone of all His treasure,
  Rest in the bottome lay.

"For if I should," said He,
"Bestow this jewell also on My creature,
He would adore My gifts in stead of Me,

And rest in Nature, not the God of Nature:
   So both should losers be.

"Yet let him keep the rest,
But keep them with repining restlessnesse;
Let him be rich and wearie, that at least,
If goodnesse leade him not, yet wearinesse
   May tosse him to My breast."

Other forms of the same desire are deplored and denounced by the perpetrators of this same religious tradition. Those who channel their desire toward God are canonized and held up as examples to follow; those who channel the same desire toward their fellow human beings are condemned. Literature issuing from the first is hagiography; the alternative is often condemned as pornography. Yet both literatures speak of the same reality — human desire. The ambiguity is already in the Bible: We can read it either way in the Song of Songs, for instance. So what? It is the same thing in two different guises. If you strip St. Augustine and Madame Bovary of their saintliness or sinfulness, you get another man and another woman trying to grapple with the same reality. Mirages that appear to thirsty people in a desert have their psychic counterparts. We must be wary of the religious solution to the problem of desire. Does such a solution mean that we maintain the basic structure — the source, the movement, the object, as these have been described, and focus these upon what we call God?

There are those who claim that each of us is bound to worship either God or some idol that is a substitute god. It matters little what this idol is. It could be a person, it could be a cause, it could be a thing. The proposers of such a view claim that all we have to do is reveal, or have revealed to us, the inadequacy of such an idol, and the movement of desire would revert automatically to the real God. This is to claim that the desire for idols is essentially the same as the desire for God; it differs only in its object. Others would claim, with Martin Buber, that "it is blasphemy when one wishes, after the idol has crashed behind the altar, to pile up an unholy sacrifice to God on the desecrated place."

Whatever the rights and the wrongs of such application of desire to God, the fact is that each of us has some relationship with the ultimate, some life of the spirit, that might come under such a heading as our "spirituality." The danger of "spirituality" is that it becomes an area in itself, cut off from "theology" on the one hand and daily life on the other. It would undertake to furnish a middle road, the "ordinary" person's way to God. We might find ourselves saying that "my" spirituality is down-to-earth; it doesn't concern itself with all that highfalutin stuff the theologians go on with, and it doesn't believe in all this modern biblical exegesis, for instance. Such a disconnected religiosity can be very comforting and "real" to me; it might have been my religious scenario from early youth; it might be an "old-time religion" (good enough for Moses, therefore good enough for me) with which I was brought up and in which I hope to die. It can surround me like an atmosphere. It is my religious "worldview." We find people saying that "their" spirituality is more optimistic than ours, which is more "Jansenistic" or "Tridentine." Or vice versa!

Individuals, pious groups, religious houses, congregations, even countries can have their own spirituality, and for the most part, this is perfectly natural, and there is no harm in it. It can happen, however, that "spirituality" takes over from theology, and we find ourselves adopting attitudes, devotions, worldviews, and beliefs that are contrary to any form of theology whatsoever. This is why "spirituality" should always hold itself open to the hardnosed research of scholars and exegetes. It should never settle for less than the truth that makes us free.

In my own case, for me as a Christian, the cross has always been a problem. Did Christ have to die on a cross? Was crucifixion necessary? What does it mean to live under the sign of the cross? When Christians bless themselves, they make the sign of the cross. Jewish blessings are not signs of a cross. Why have we made this equivalence of blessing and crucifixion? "By your Holy Cross you have redeemed the world," we say in the Easter Liturgy. If he had died in a gas chamber or had been executed by a firing squad, would he not have redeemed the world?

And I have always found it difficult to accept the usual depictions of the crucifixion in most Roman Catholic churches, especially the standard pictures representing the so-called fourteen stations of the cross. These are presented like pseudo-realistic colored photographs of an effeminate-looking Jesus, dressed as if for tennis, with a halo and a wistful, otherworldly pained expression, while tear-stricken women, usually in blue, crawl behind him, and monstrous soldiers, of the sadistic war-movie genre, take evident delight in inflicting as much cruel pain as possible on their wimpish victim.

As a child I was told incredible and contradictory accounts of what happened: On the one hand, because he was God, Jesus knew exactly what was going to happen to him, and it was the preview movie in the Garden of Gethsemane that caused him to sweat blood. When he was on the cross, he could see the whole world and the complete unfolding of history to the extent and detail that he could even see me, urchin that I was, and every misdemeanor of mine was an added source of pain to him. On the other hand, he, like Captain Marvel in the comics, could have knocked those soldiers out cold, or popped the nails out of his feet and driven them into their eyes, but he didn't choose to do that. He restrained himself as God, and submitted himself as man, to this gruesome ceremony. And all for my puny sake, to show me how dreadfully he was being treated by everyone, including me. Well, when the story was told this way, I always wished that he hadn't bothered.

Another theory was that the Roman soldiers had invented crucifixion for the purpose of inflicting maximum torture on this particular victim (presumably because he was God) and that he, because of his divine nature, had such a heightened sensitivity that every part of the execution process hurt him thousands of times more than it would have hurt any other mere human being. And this was why the cross was a saving instrument. It produced the most excruciating pain ever endured in human history, and the waves of this redemptive pain reached to the ends of the earth and of time, like death-rays to sin. The cross produced a kind of chemotherapy that devastated the cancer of evil and death.

It came as a surprise to me to find out that crucifixion was one of the official methods of execution at that time and that thousands were killed in this way, even to the extent, on one occasion, of lining both sides of the Appian Way with crucified bodies.

This all boils down to a certain understanding, or misunderstanding, of what actually happened in history, and an interpretation of God that each person weaves out of a common basket of threads. Christians would hold that they at least have one source of knowledge, and therefore of spirituality, that is guaranteed and unimpeachable — the Holy Bible. We have four eyewitness accounts, they say, of what happened and divinely inspired interpretations of each event.

My experience is of the same amount and kind of ambiguity here — a plethora of "spiritualities" spawned from one apparently pristine and unequivocal source. Let me give a concrete example. There are people who have a great devotion to what they regard as the seven last words spoken by Jesus from the cross. Hermeneutics and demythologization be damned, they are sure that the phrases uttered by Jesus as he was dying could not have been made up by anyone and must be direct speech from the Godman himself. They weave a tapestry of these final utterances of Christ:

> "Father, forgive them, for they know not what they do."

> "Woman, behold thy son! . . . Behold thy Mother."

> "Truly I say to you, this day you will be with me in Paradise."

> "*Eli, Eli, lama sabachthani*" (My God, my God, why have you forsaken me?)

> "I thirst."

> "It is accomplished."

> "Father, into Thy hands I commend my Spirit."

They imagine that from these direct quotations we get a very clear picture of what happened to Jesus on the day of his crucifixion, that there was a very efficient secretary at the foot of the cross who took down verbatim everything he said. This is the kind of simplification that "spirituality" can impose upon exegesis, in a way that, from the outset, compromises the "truth."

To explain what I understand to be the "hermeneutical" problem we face when reading such scriptures or any other text, let me juxtapose two diaries of events. The first would be a skeletal account of the first hundred years of the history of cinema, stretching from 1896 to 1996.

The second is the more or less established time frame, which a consensus of biblical scholarship presents, to date the composition of the texts that we now refer to as the Christian scriptures. This would take us from the year 50 CE to three hundred years later when the canon was closed. There was a timespan of about a hundred years between the birth of Jesus and the composition of the final texts of this canon: 6 BCE–96 CE.

What I am trying to create is a parallel situation in our own experience that will allow us to understand what happened in this context two thousand years ago.

Cinema is an art form, a medium, that did not exist before the twentieth century. From the beginning, it was used to express, in its own way, the mystery and the meaning of the life and death of Jesus Christ. Two years after it is said to have actually begun in 1897, the Lumière Society in France showed a film called *The Passion*. I, who entered the century only halfway through, remember the premiere screening of Cecil B. de Mille's *The Ten Commandments* in 1956 and *The King of Kings* in 1961. However, these were only the remakes in color. Those who are a quarter of a century older than myself will remember the first black-and-white versions in 1923 and 1924 respectively. In 1966 we were shown *The Bible*, no less, which was billed as "the authentic film of the book." All these were attempts to use the techniques and magic of cinema to portray what the director believed to be the reality of God's appearance among us.

So there was trick photography and signs and wonders that only the cinema can produce. The crossing of the Red Sea was a tour de force, and the Ten Commandments were hewn in granite, accompanied by thunder and lightning on the mountainside. Unfortunately, a jet plane flew over at the time of filming, and one of the commandments was left out, but it was too expensive to do a retake. These intrusions and omissions will remain forever parts of these human accounts.

In the 1965 film *The Greatest Story Ever Told*, John Wayne was the centurion standing at the foot of the cross. When Christ died, every creativity that the cinema could muster showed the awfulness of the event. There was darkness and storms, and the renting of the temple veil, and thunder and lightning. John Wayne's line was: "Truly this was the Son of God." Apparently George Stevens, who had directed his most famous movie, *Shane*, with Alan Ladd, was not happy with Wayne's performance: "For heaven's sake, John," he urged, "will you put a bit of awe into it." So John Wayne extrapolated: "Aw, truly this was the Son of God." The point being that artists who feel called upon to tell the greatest story ever told use their imagination to convey what they regard as the most important parts of it; they do their best to put some awe into it, especially when an event has supernatural repercussions that are not always evident from the purely historical narrative.

So let me take at random four cinematic gospels: in 1964 *The Gospel according to St. Matthew* by Pier Paolo Pasolini; in 1975 *The Messiah* of Roberto Rossellini; in 1977 *Jesus of Nazareth* by Franco Zeffirelli, and in 1988 Martin Scorsese's *The Last Temptation of Christ*. The first thing to note is that there is nearly a quarter of a century between the first film here and the last. Today, however, you can rent or purchase a video and have these versions on your screen whenever you wish. When Zeffirelli's film was shown on television on Palm Sunday and Easter Sunday of the Year of Our Lord 1977, it was a six-hour show that kept twenty-one million viewers glued to their TV screens. If you missed it, that was it.

Martin Scorsese's interpretation, on the other hand, caused such a scandal that his film was banned in many countries. This embargo aroused huge — and, aficionados would hold, unwarranted — interest among the sensation-hungry public. Long queues formed outside the cinemas, braving the moral ire of the righteous, who formed corresponding queues of protesters on the other side, praying for the souls of those being led into *The Last Temptation*. So my second point is that each of these four is entirely different. The gospel according to Pasolini is a Marxist interpretation of the text. Zeffirelli's is a highly "traditional" presentation. And the tradition is that of Western European art, evoking in his images Memling, Brueghel, El Greco, and Piero della Francesca. "Here we see a Herod the Great worthy of Rembrandt, a blind beggar straight out of Brueghel, a St. Matthew in the best sense Caravaggesque, a Last Supper that could be some incredible lost masterpiece by Georges de la Tour."[1]

So what I am asking you to imagine is that two hundred years from now, the church might decide that out of all the films about the life of Christ, four were going to be selected as the definitive presentation, as the authoritative statement, as the canonical version of the greatest story ever told. The faithful of that Year of Our Lord 2200 would be in a situation similar to their predecessors when the New Testament was finally closed, which happened 250 years after the events recorded there. And the Christians of the year 4000 would be in a situation similar to the one we find ourselves in today, when faced with the seven texts purporting to be the last words from the cross. In order to understand Pasolini, we would have to know something of the Marxist philosophy that so dominated the century we have just been through, and that will be quite forgotten by then. In order to understand Zeffirelli, we would have to know the visual quotations he is making from a tradition of sacred art, dating back to Giotto in the thirteenth century and ending with Caravaggio in the sixteenth. In order to understand *The Last Temptation of Christ,* we would have to know that it was based upon a previous text written by Greek novelist Nikos Kazantzakis. Without this contextual information, it would be difficult to understand why the particular director presented the story of Jesus in the way he did.

My problem with the seven so-called last utterances of Jesus on the cross is somewhat similar. The texts do not come from any one film. They are taken out of four different versions. Out of context and in the new sequence, they form a composite text. They create an illusion.

The century after the death of Jesus witnessed a proliferation of attempts to tell the greatest story ever told. These ranged from gnostic mythologies to historical romances. One of the former would tell us that Christ was actually up a tree laughing at the crucifixion, that a substitute had been put in at the last minute; Simon of Cyrene usually got the credit for being the stunt artist. The second kind included tales of Jesus being revived in the tomb (having taken a magic potion that made it look as if he were dead) and running off with Mary Magdalene, usually to India, sometimes to Marseilles. Such "traditions" abounded. Now, they didn't have videos and they didn't have books. We are inclined to forget that the proliferation of pocket editions of the Bible is a phenomenon of the twentieth century. The *Book of Kells* required no less than the slaughter of 185 calves to provide the "paper" on which it was penned with arsenic and sulfur. And that was five hundred years after the century we are talking about. So all these traditions were oral, and they varied from place to place, from one church assembly to another.

In the book that we now call the New Testament, half a century separates the texts of St. Paul (who never met the historical Jesus) and the writings attributed to St. John (known as the beloved disciple): Eighty years of mulling over the meaning, of understanding what really did happen, separates the death of Jesus and the appearance of the fourth gospel as we now have it. The crucified Jesus makes three statements in John and three in Luke. None of these are the same and none of them corresponds to the one statement attributed to Matthew/Mark. It appears that John regarded the version provided by Matthew/Mark as too pessimistic. Theirs has been described as "low" christology. That Jesus would have asked for this chalice to pass from his lips and would have felt himself abandoned on the cross — such thoughts are inimical to the "high" christology of the Johannine text.

What all seem to agree upon is that Jesus died "in accordance with the scriptures" (1 Cor. 15:3). The problem is: Which scripture texts do you refer to? In the Gospel of Luke it is quite clear that the soldiers offer Jesus vinegar to drink in fulfillment of the text (Ps. 69): "In my thirst they gave me vinegar to drink," which emphasizes the suffering servant and the humiliation inflicted upon him. For John, the "I thirst" seems to be almost a corrective to that pessimism about the Passion. John is portraying Jesus as "thirsting" for the chalice that his Father has asked him to drink. Thus the wine that is given him to drink is not at all a kind of insult on the part of the soldiers. In fact, in this text, we do not even know that it is a soldier who offers it. It says "they," and the last people referred to are his mother and St. John. The reason why Jesus says "I thirst" is because he knows that the scriptures have to be fulfilled. He thirsts for this fulfillment.

This fulfillment is accomplished in the drinking of the chalice.

The wine here mentioned is not vinegar but the equivalent of some *vin ordinaire* that would have been drunk by soldiers. Plutarch, in his life of Cato Maior, says of him that "water was what he drank on campaigns, but occasionally in a raging thirst he would request this vinegary wine," which is the same word used by John (*oxos*). So when we take the composite text, rather than any particular gospel, we imagine that the phrase "I thirst" used by St. John, for instance, was an indication of further torture for Jesus, and that the nasty Roman soldier, when he asked for a drink, went to the sadistic trouble of giving him vinegar or destroying the nice wine he was drinking himself by deliberately pouring vinegar or gall into it. This is not the case, as a more objective exegesis would present it. Such an interpretation is out of context and goes against the thrust of John's theology. Jesus, for John, says "I thirst" in order that the scriptures should be fulfilled, so that "they" would give him the wine of salvation to drink. He died of his own accord, at the time appointed, and only after he had completed everything that had been given him to do. He is totally in control of his life and his death. "Whatever the Johannine Jesus does or says flows from what he saw with the Father before his incarnation and, indeed, before the world began" (John 5:19; 8:28; 17:5).[2]

John's account does not have the "awe" in it that the synoptics have: They go in for apocalyptic elements such as darkness, the loud cry, earthquakes, and the rending of the veil in the temple. John is more down-to-earth and factual. He wants each detail to be presented as the enactment of a scene already discussed and prepared by the Trinity before the world began. When the soldiers divided up the clothes of Jesus in the way they did, it was because they, without knowing it, were subject to the all-powerful orchestration of the Son of God on the cross. They may have thought that they were crucifying him, that they were killing him, but, in fact, they were unconscious acolytes in a religious ceremony. He was laying down his life in a specific ritual that was preordained, every detail of which had been foretold in the scriptures. The quotation "I thirst" is of a similar order and is uttered to achieve their response, which is to put the wine to his lips so that he might drink it to the last. In this perspective, the early Christians regarded the death of Jesus as miraculous. Tertullian, for instance, explains that Jesus "with a word expressing his own will dismissed his spirit, forestalling the work of the executioners."[3]

When John says that they did not break his legs, that they pierced his side and blood and water poured forth, he is thinking of the fulfillment of the scriptures and the inauguration of the new era of the eucharistic kingdom. He is not taking a literal or a scientific point of view. Nor would anyone have done so at that time. Nobody believed that God died of a heart attack. That was left to our own times to introduce. In fact, the first discussion of the death of Jesus as a physiological issue was in the nineteenth century, when it was proposed that Jesus died from a violent rupture of the heart. After hemorrhaging had taken place through the heart wall into the pericardial sac, it was said there was a clotting of blood separating it from serum. The lance would then have opened the pericardial sac, releasing two substances that appeared as blood and water. Add this to the shroud of Turin, and you are on your way to a whole theology and spirituality of gloom and doom. Our Lord died of a broken heart caused by his vision of human ingratitude and our sins.

We have to be careful not to read into the text our particular concerns, the hang-ups of our own spiritual pathology, or cultural fashions of the times and places in which we live. We must try to establish as nearly as we can what the author of the text had in mind.

The fact that an evangelist is inspired does not make him any less a human person. John must have been a poet, a theologian, a great lover and mystic. His Christ was the king of glory. There is no point in looking at another gospel to elaborate his thought, because the gospel traditions are different. Far from being either a scandalous or a diminishing realization, for me this is an enrichment and a challenge. It means that from the very beginning there were different denominations, different theologies, different ways of telling the greatest story ever told. And these are already contained in the New Testament. There were Orthodox, Catholic, and Protestant traditions in the church from its inception. The New

Testament is an ecumenical document. It contains variety and healthy tension between traditions issuing from different churches, which articulated the vision of Christ as this was handed down to each of them.

> The vision of Christ which thou dost see
> Is my vision's greatest enemy:
> Thine has a great hooked nose like thine,
> Mine has a snub-nose like to mine:
> Both read our Bible day and night,
> But thou read'st black where I read white.
>
> *William Blake*[4]

Above all, the truth we believe in is a person, not a book. A living person. We "do" this in remembrance of him. We do not just read it. When the word of God is read out in the assembly during our celebration of the Lord's Passover, it speaks to each of us personally. "I thirst" is God speaking to us as desire. I find no parallel in other gospel texts. The only account that comes near to approximating it is the following about the death of the great Muslim mystic Al Hallaj, on March 26, 922, in Baghdad. This sublime ecstatic was condemned to death by the jurists of his own religion because, in the exaltation of his ecstasy, he made himself equal to God and thereby broke the golden commandment, the *Shahadah:* that there is no God but God.

> His hands and feet were cut off, after he had received five hundred lashes. He besmeared his face

with his bleeding stumps, whether to hide his pallor or to perform the ritual ablutions for the last time in his own blood. Then he was fastened to the cross, and I, his son Hamd, heard him conversing with God in ecstasy on the gibbet.... When evening fell, the caliph's messengers brought authority for him to be beheaded. But they said: It is too late, let us put it off till tomorrow. When the morning came, he was taken down from the gibbet and brought forward so that his head might be smitten off. And I heard him cry out and say in a very loud voice: what the ecstatic desires is the Sole One, alone with Him![5]

This text, written by the victim's son, has something of the same ring as the account of St. John. It is the thirst of the mystic for union with God, for return to the Father. Jesus was just about to accomplish the greatest breakthrough in the history of the world. This was *The Dambusters March* and "The Battle Hymn of the Republic." In his own body he was about to complete the most wonderful irrigation system that creation had ever witnessed. He was about to unleash the flood of divine compassion and love into the mainstream, the bloodstream of humanity. Because he trampled the grapes and drank the wine of redemption to the dregs, his wounded body became the source of life from which blood and water flowed. He thirsts for this accomplishment.

This is very different from other "spiritualities" of the crucifixion. In fact, the strange truth it seems to be suggesting is that the crucifixion was an act that produced the resurrection of the body in Christ almost as an orgasm of love, that the nearest approximation and analogy we might have at our disposal to even hint at the nature of this particular bodily act is the sexual one. The emergence of new life, the generation of new birth, the resurrection from the dead, find most appropriate analogies in the human way of transmitting life. Nor has the way in which God saves humankind and wins over each one of us ever lacked sexual imagery. *Erexit cornu salutis* (He erected a horn of salvation) is the Latin version of the Benedictus Canticle that Luke puts in the mouth of Zachary, father of John the Baptist, when he hears the good news of salvation.

Everything about the crucifixion speaks of penetration of the body — the scourging, piercing, crowning with thorns, driving of nails into the hands and feet. It is a searching out, as Psalm 138 puts it: "My body held no secret from you." The very psalm that Christ is meant to have uttered on the cross says: "They tear holes in my hands and my feet" and asks to be saved from "the horns of these oxen." All of which conspires to present the crucifixion as a breaking of the body to allow divine power to flow through. And the words "I thirst" are a positive expression of that *manikon eros*, that crazy desire that God has had for human beings since the beginning of the world.

Chapter Five

GOD'S CRACKPOT LOVE

W HEN WE RELATE TO GOD, the same conditions apply as we encountered in scriptural exegesis. We have to stay with it until all our projections, our hatreds, our expectations, our presuppositions and preconceived ideas, our silly impressions, our caricatures, our holy pictures, have dissolved, and we are groping in the darkness for the unassuming, inarticulate nonentity at the other end of the line. As in all other relations, love transforms desire to meet the reality of the other. In this case the other is God, and sometimes this reality proves such a shock to our system that we imagine we are involved with some kind of sadist or tyrant.

I have translated the Greek words *manikon eros* into "crackpot love" for assonantal as well as descriptive reasons: It is a crazy kind of love. The whole of heaven is laughing at God's ridiculous infatuation with the least likely of creatures. In a film called *Pigsty* Pasolini describes a man who falls in love with the pigs housed in the farmyard on his father's magnificent estate. This unfortunate "pigophile" has to creep off to the pigsty whenever he can reach it unobserved, to indulge his shameful passion. When the gruesome truth of what is happening dawns on his family, they are mortified and unable to accept the degradation and disgrace to themselves. The film is a symbol of a kind of loving beyond the bounds of credibility and acceptability.

In something of the same outraged reprehension, angels and archangels seem to have deplored the amorous connection between God and his chosen ones among the people of Israel. The book of Job describes one attempt on their part to discredit this unworthy object of God's love and God's trembling trust in Job to be faithful to his love in the face of all adversity. However, even the chosen people joined the disapproving fray at the suggestion that God would actually become a human being to show his love and to win ours. As well as being folly to the Greeks, this was also scandal to the Jews. But, in the end, it was proof, as St. Paul says, of the height and the depth, the length and the breadth of God's love for us as human beings.

Since the dawn of human consciousness we have been projecting our fantasies onto the screen we call God. Great rabbis have suggested that the Bible can be as much an anthropology for God as a theology for us. It tells the story of our projections and God's attempts to purify these throughout the history of the relationship between himself and the Jewish people. We have distorted, even villainized this love. Much literature is an expression of these projected fantasies. Emily Brontë, for instance, in describing the famous love affair between Cathy and Heathcliff, is giving some insight into her own relationship with the God of *Wuthering Heights*. Cathy marries Linton and loves him also in another way, but her love at the deep end is for Heathcliff:

> My great thought in living is himself [Heathcliff]. If all else perished, and *he* remained, I should still continue to be; and if all else remained, and he were annihilated, the universe would turn to a mighty stranger: I should not seem a part of it. My love for Linton is like the foliage in the woods: time will change it, I'm well aware, as winter changes the trees — my love for Heathcliff resembles the eternal rocks beneath — a source of little visible delight, but necessary. Nelly, I *am* Heathcliff — he's always, always in my mind — not as a pleasure, any more than I am always a pleasure to myself — but, as my own being.[1]

We recognize the vocabulary and the cadence of this famous declaration of Cathy's love for Heathcliff in the mystical poem that Emily Brontë wrote about her own relationship with God:

> No coward soul is mine
> No trembler in the world's storm-troubled sphere

I see Heaven's glories shine
And Faith shines equal arming me from Fear.

O God within my breast
Almighty ever-present Deity
Life, that in me hast rest
As I, Undying Life, have power in thee.

. . . .

So surely anchored on
The steadfast rock of Immortality.

. . . .

Though earth and moon were gone,
And suns and universes ceased to be
And thou wert left alone
Every Existence would exist in thee.[2]

According to the doctrine of the Trinity, God lives as a mystery of love among persons.[3] God exists as an eternal exchange of love between persons. We are invited to share this personal love, which means a kind of loving that unites us with the three divine persons. Their lifestyle is a mutual giving and receiving, a ceremony of reciprocity. The word in Greek is *perichoresis*. The Greeks have two words for a place: *topos* and *chora*. *Topos* is a place as a location; *chora* is a place you know, an intimate place, like home or a private scene where you feel you have roots (*peri* + *chora* = round this space). It is within such a loving space that the three divine persons infiltrate one another reciprocally, without invasion. We are offered access to this delicate household.

The ultimate theological error or heresy is thinking of God as living in an altogether different sphere from us without any possible contact. Since the incarnation of God the Son, we share the same household. We are children of this household. Although we cannot be divine by nature, we have become so by adoption. This is a problem, as it is for many adopted children — to really believe that we are part of the household. It is, however, *our* problem. God has gone to infinite pains to assure us of this fact. And such involvement has also made a difference to the Trinity of persons, who in some strange way are more fully themselves by this multiple outlet for their self-giving love.

In the end it is not our love for God but God's love for us that is the initiating and formative part of our mutual relationship. It must be clear to us by now that God is not an all-powerful dictator, not an omniscient ogre, not a sadistic tyrant. The prepersonal concepts of God, inherited mostly from Greek philosophy, are bankrupt in the light of God's own revelation of himself. And the love of the Trinity, depending as it does on our free acceptance at each moment, has had to be the most ingenious salvage operation ever imagined. At each stubborn refusal to cooperate, at each fearful rejection of what is on offer, at every willful decision to throw away the lifeline, the three persons in pursuit have had to regroup and rearrange their strategy.

God, as hound of heaven, comes after us. We have to be fully aware that God loves us, hungers for us, needs us. Half the story of our relationship with him is the result of his relentless refusal to allow us to give up on him. He has tried every way possible to show us this love. Eventually he sent his only begotten son. Jesus is the human face of God: "Whoever has seen me has seen the Father." Jesus shows us who God is through his personality and through his every action from birth to death. These include his childhood, his adolescence, his adulthood; his living seminar on love encompasses every social situation, every tiny communication, every human relationship. He is the living embodiment of God. The disciples were captivated by what they saw, what they heard, what they touched. St. John, particularly, never stops telling us how some kind of lightning flashed through this man that would make you adore him, compel you to become his disciple. Wilhelm Reich suggests that, from a purely human standpoint, attractiveness is caused mostly by the relaxed quality of a person's musculature, which is the result of flowing psychic agility: "The rhythmicity of one's movements, the alternation of muscular tension and relaxation in movement, go together with the capacity for linguistic modulation and general musicality. In such people, one has the feeling of direct psychic contact."[4]

Whether we ascribe this attraction to the sexuality of Jesus or to charism, the seductiveness and enthrallment of his bodily reality are undeniable. Napoleon Bonaparte, writing from exile, claimed to be the greatest person who had ever lived on this planet. However, he realized that

his influence over people was dependent upon his physical presence. (He said that if persons were standing
in his presence he could get them to do anything he
wanted them to do. This was proved by his arrival from
exile onto French soil, when he immediately attracted
even the soldiery sent to oppose him to join his cause.)
The only person greater than himself, he said, was Jesus
Christ, who could exercise a similar influence long after
he was dead.

Such an influence is ambiguous. In his film *Theorema,*
Pasolini shows the arrival of an angel (Terence Stamp)
in an ordinary household. He seduces every member of
the family in turn — the maid, the son, the father, the
mother, and the daughter. Then he leaves. That is the
first part of the theorem (the title of the film means "theorem" in Italian, but the word might also be divided into
the Greek roots *theos* and *rema,* meaning God's word).[5]
In the second part of the theorem each bereft member
of the family adopts a perverse and extravagant career
as a result of the disorienting connection with the alien
lover. The mother pursues young male students at the
local university. The maid has visions and levitations and
becomes the center of a mystico-erotic cult. The daughter is struck down with chronic anemia and wastes away.
The son becomes an unsuccessful artist. The father takes
off all his clothes on the platform of a railway station
and walks into the public lavatories in pursuit of some
look-alike of the visiting angel. As he enters through the
doorway, the scene changes and he is walking through a

vast desert with vultures flying overhead. The subtitles quote the prophet Jeremiah, who complains of being seduced by God and led into the desert: "You have seduced me, Yahweh, and I have let myself be seduced; you have overpowered me: you were the stronger" (Jer. 20:7).

God becoming man in Jesus Christ could be a tantalizing seducer who leaves us worse off than before he came, unless the Third Person of the Trinity intervenes to shift the focus of attraction and bring us back to earth within ourselves. The Holy Spirit is God indwelling in our particular personhood. We are the body of Christ because of his assumption of our nature, his body-and-blood reality, as one of us. But each of us is what Jesus Christ was, and each of us is now where Jesus Christ is for all eternity, through the ingenuity of the Holy Spirit. This is the meaning of the mystery of the Ascension — Jesus leaving the disciples so that we find God in ourselves. They had no sense of the new kind of personhood we are invited to become. They were grieving for him, looking up into the sky, until an angel was sent to tell them to focus on the earth, to focus on ourselves. Jesus Christ's humanity, his mission, his blessing, can be accomplished only by his leaving us in body and returning to us in person. This internal Christ consciousness is induced in us by his moving upward.

He leaves them, the scriptures tell us, in a ritual, a liturgy, a blessing, which is the *ite missa est* itself (Go, you are dismissed), in its new personality. "As he said this, he was lifted up while they looked on." What was he saying while he was lifted up? He was telling them that they would each receive the Holy Spirit, not as a conflagration but as an individual tongue of fire merging into the flame and the quick of each individual person's life. They cannot receive this Holy Spirit until he, as bodily presence, goes and leaves them. He is in the way. They are traumatized by him. The accomplishment, fulfillment, perfection of this intoxicating relationship is for him to go, so that they can find themselves when left to themselves. The Holy Spirit is God indwelling in themselves and not God incarnate in him.

Life with and in the Holy Spirit makes us persons in the fullest sense of the word, which is as spoken by the Persons of the Trinity itself. We become a new creation, a combination of humanity and divinity, which is the ultimate in creativity on both sides of the border between God and us. We allow divinity to penetrate our being in "bright shoots of everlastingness," as Henry Vaughan describes the effect. Teilhard de Chardin suggests that contemplatives can change the orientation of humanity: "The contemplative is an energy center for humanity."

The Holy Spirit makes us members of a new species, "living from the religious center of personal energy where spiritual emotions are the habitual core." Such was the scientific observation of William James a hundred years ago in his attempt to describe the varieties of religious experience.[6] The new creation, the new kind of humanity, develops its own particular intensity of passion, its own kind of emotional life. When a certain intensity is attained by the new emotion, "the new ardor which burns in his breast consumes in its glow the lower 'uses' which formerly beset him, and keeps him immune against infection from the entire groveling portion of his nature." What James calls "the expulsive power of a higher affection"[7] deals with the natural mechanism of our possessive and infatuated relationships. This happens by a "conversion," a change of currency, a removal of one fuse and its replacement by another. "To get to it, a critical point must usually be passed, a corner turned within one. Something must give way, a native hardness must break down and liquefy."[8]

So the other meaning of crackpot love is more literal. We are made of dust and earth, made as vessels of clay, as pots thrown by an almighty potter. The effect of his love on us is to break the potbound periphery and open us out through the cracks. We have to be broken open. The walls have to be razed. We have to be ploughed like earth being prepared for sowing. The passion of individualism, which is instinctually in our nature as an ontological necessity of self-preservation, self-promotion, and self-fulfillment, has to be superseded by the passion of ecstasy, the movement of exodus that pours us out into the space between us and other people, accomplishing in us the movement that makes us capable of real love, *capax Dei*. We are born individuals; we become persons by this expansion of ourselves into the antechamber of the other. We have to do for ourselves

what God has already done for himself in our regard —
break out of our natural mode of being and ensure that
our nature no longer determines the limits of our personhood. This extract from Norman Nicholson's poem "The
Pot Geranium" provides an image that describes what
can happen:

> A box-kite rides the air, a square of calico,
> Crimson as the cornets of the Royal
>   Temperance Band
> . . . .
>   I turn from the window . . .
> And lie on my bed. The ceiling
> Slopes over like a tent, and white walls
> Wrap themselves round me, leaving only
> A flap for the light to blow through. Thighs and
>   spine
> Are clamped to the mattress and looping springs
> Twine round my chest and hold me. I feel the air
> Move on my face like spiders, see the light
> Slide across the plaster; but the wind and sun
> Are mine no longer, nor have I kite to claim them,
> Or string to fish the clouds. But there on a shelf
> In the warm corner of my dormer window
> A pot geranium flies its bright balloon,
> Nor can the festering hot-house of the tropics
> Breed a tenser crimson, for this crock of soil,
> Six inches deep by four across,
> Contains the pattern, the prod and pulse of life,

Complete as the Nile or the Niger.
    And what need therefore
To stretch for the straining kite? — for kite and
    flower
Bloom in my room forever; the light that lifts them
Shines in my own eyes, and my body's warmth
Hatches their red in my veins. It is the Gulf Stream
That rains down the chimney, making the soot
    spit; it is the Trade Wind
That blows in the draught under the bedroom door.
My ways are circumscribed, confined as a limpet
To one small radius of rock; yet
I eat the equator, breathe the sky, and carry
The great white sun in the dirt of my finger-nails.[9]

The ways in which we burst the bonds of our circum-scribed insularity and open ourselves outward toward radiating energy are many and varied. The most effective and appropriate crash course toward personhood depends on the kind of individual we are. I once saw an hour-long documentary interview with the cinema director Ingmar Bergman. Here is a man whose nature is so wild, whose love is so intense, whose passion is so devouring that his unmediated presence to a world of people would produce relationships that burn up and disintegrate like dry leaves in a furnace. He had to find some complicated cooling structure and allow "the other" to come into contact with him without being destroyed.

89

The mediating texture that both united him to, and protected him from, a world with whom he demanded an intimacy that penetrated like acid was the cinema — the creative web of relationships that produces films. Through this highly technical and, at the same time, spontaneous and uniquely personal liturgy, he found, or rather created, the structure that allowed him to express and to receive that concentrated interest and communion that would have been impossible for him and for anyone who loved him without the detonating network of filmmaking. In this way, the "too much" of an overheated passion is not doomed to the frustration of impotence; it can be creatively extended and diversified into an ensemble, a community, that does not expect the passion to be focused upon it, but that can allow it to explode into myriad different particles, corresponding to a multitude of different people.

The question "How do you make a film, Mr. Bergman?" is a false one. It is placing the film at the level of productivity and searching for someone who caused it to be. There is no single cause of his films, least of all Bergman himself. And they do not occur at the level of productivity; they happen as an extension of his own being, his personality. He says: "I enjoy making films. They are a wonderful way for a person like me ... to have fruitful contact with people." He is the one through whom the film happens. He is the ground, the occasion, the unique person through whom this wealth of talent, personality, and human search for meaning finds a form and a way of crystallizing. He is the subtle coagulator of the flux of relations.

Without him the film would not be made, and yet he is not the creator of the film. It is the blend of talent and personality that forms this community and allows this happening to take place. Not one of the people working on this film could produce it without him. Each one of them contributes the selfhood and the personality that must flow together through the prism of Bergman's receptivity into a final shape that expresses the happening adequately. This is Bergman's way of meeting. His personality demands the combination of intimacy and creativity to bring out the genius of his unusual being. The film is the structural extension of his being-in-the-world; that is also why so many of his films are about human communication. The film is the third term, the setting and the structure that allow otherwise destructive and antagonistic forces to coexist — not just to unite and preserve each in its specific identity, but to invent a new mode of existence in the film itself as a work of art. So art can be the medium through which we develop individuality into personhood.

Solzhenitsyn, another twentieth-century artist, tells us how the concentration camps in Russia had a similar effect on him. His novels are almost eulogies of the unforeseen benefits, in terms of personality development and religious awareness, that Russian communism unwittingly bestowed upon those dissidents who refused to conform to its requirements. In spite of itself, the communist regime helped Russians to reach new dimensions of their being within the inhuman conditions designed to reintegrate them into the architecture of totalitarianism. The horrific circumstances that produced in Solzhenitsyn his new birth into such dimensions were the three great scourges of the twentieth century — war, cancer, and the concentration camps. These formed for him the inexorable straitjacket that forced him to find "the first circle" of himself, which is the place where we come into contact with what he describes as "some unknown source of strength."

We do not have to be led to these inestimable riches, this other dimension at the Point Zero of ourselves, by the external imposition of tragic circumstances. To pluck this note from the forgotten realm and play it over and over again is to live the monotony of being. To stay willingly and obstinately in this place (stability), refusing to allow anything to come between us and the reality of what we are (humility), dispossessing ourselves of all else (poverty), so that we can listen to the mystery of being (obedience) — such is another way of structuring intimacy and channeling passion that is monastic life. This option can be described as a creative concentration camp. It is an attempt to reconstruct on earth the household of God.

But, again, this is an unusual way. For most people, the way from individuality to personhood is the way of "love." We are dragged toward fulfillment of this potential for otherness, which is in each of us, by the harrowing fire of love. Love is the only impetus that is sufficiently overwhelming to force us to leave the comfortable shelter of our well-armored individuality, shed the impregnable shell of self-sufficiency, and crawl out nakedly into the danger zone beyond, the melting-pot where individuality is purified into personhood.

Chapter Six

THE WAY
THROUGH THE
WANDERING ROCKS

Jerzy Skolimowski, the Polish director, made a film called *Deep End* in English in 1970. It was a most striking parable about love as a crucible of personhood.

The film is about a boy of fifteen who leaves school and gets his first job as male attendant in an indoor public swimming pool. There is a girl attendant also who shows him the ropes. The film primarily takes place around the big rectangular swimming pool, where people of all ages come to bathe — mostly at the shallow end.

The boy is quickly initiated into the reality that most of the clients don't bother about the pool at all but come to the changing rooms to gratify themselves in every way imaginable. He is sent by one fat lady (Diana Dors) to fetch her medicated shampoo. When he returns, she wants him to help her undress. He flees when they get to her bra. After her shower she faints and rings for him. Then she begins to "play football" with him — pressing his head into her breasts. The next time a client asks him to fetch shampoo, he pushes it under the door and takes to his heels.

He becomes aware that the girl attendant (Jane Asher) is performing various off-duty calls in the different rooms. One sporty fellow is in charge of a large bevy of schoolgirls. They wear expansive bathing costumes and are lined up against the back wall terrified of the plunge into freezing water. He, wearing a very tight T-shirt, blows a whistle and picks out various pleading victims, whom he pinches on the bottom and slaps into the pool. He marches round like a prancing sultan inflicting pain on the trembling and tittering mob of girlhood. He then retires to have more stimulating contact with Jane Asher in the changing room.

Soon the boy falls in love with the girl attendant. She is hard and cynical. She alternately encourages his advances and cruelly rebuffs them. When his mother and father come to have an "official" bath in "his" pool, he begs the girl to be "nice to me mum." She calls his mum an old cow. By such tactics she works the boy up into a frenzied knot of passion and frustration.

She is to be engaged to a sallow youth who takes her to see pornographic films. The infatuated boy follows them around. She backs her car onto his bicycle and generally crushes him, as when she has him removed from cinemas for indecent assault. Her lover buys her a diamond ring, which she takes great pleasure in displaying to her

infatuated slave: "How much would you say it's worth —
come on, come on, how much would you say?"

One day while she is standing outside in the snow
waiting for her lover boy number two (the elderly pincher)
to finish organizing some athletic event, the boy surprises
her. They have a fight in the snow. She punches him in the
face and knocks out one of his teeth, which falls into the
snow. He feels his mouth with his tongue. No blood. And
all his teeth are present and unbroken. It wasn't his tooth.

It was the diamond from her ring that fell into the
snow. She is horrified and paralyzed. He tells her to stand
where she is and not to move. He draws a circle around
her, and they both collect all the snow in that area and
pack it into two huge cellophane bags. They carry these
inside to the pool, which has been emptied for the week-
end, and they begin to boil small quantities of the snow
in an electric kettle, hoping to discover the diamond.
The girl removes her tights and they pour the melted
snow through these down the drain. She is in a filthy
mood. When her fiancé rings her, she says she will be
with him in an hour or so. While she is on the tele-
phone, the boy finds the diamond. When she gets back
to the pool, she finds him lying on the floor of the pool
wrapped in cellophane and rags. She pulls these from him
in fury. He is lying there naked. He opens his mouth, and
she sees the diamond lying on his tongue. "Don't swallow it. Don't swallow it!" In a frenzy she whips off her
clothes; she understands the blackmail. When she ap-
proaches, he hands her the diamond. She whips it away

from him, puts it in her bag, and begins to storm off to dress. She looks over at him helplessly curled up, humiliated. She goes to him and lies with him. There is a beautiful shot taken from the roof, looking down over them in the middle of the big empty, shoddy pool.

She gets up. The phone is ringing; it is her lover again. She is about to leave and she goes down into the pool again to collect her clothes. He can't let her go like that. Not after what has happened. They must talk. She must just stay for a bit, please. He is frantic. The pool begins to fill with water, and she begins to climb the steps. He grabs a lowered trapeze of lights and pushes it with all his strength. It swings toward her and hits her on the nape of the neck. She slumps back into the water. There is blood in the water, and the pool is full. The last image is from underwater. He is clinging to her dead body, with blood streaming from her mouth.

Love is like a swimming pool, the film seems to be saying. It has a shallow and a deep end. Those who play around in the shallow end are likely to lose their capacity ever to reach the deep, just as a diamond can be lost in snow. At the deep end love is as strong as death.

We are our bodies. We are sexual beings. Our sexuality is like yeast in bread; we are not ourselves without it. Mysticism that denies, belittles, escapes from, or ignores the body is unacceptable. It is, and always has been, true that human beings in the image of God are created male and female, and without the unity of these two there can be no redemption of our humanity. Any living out of our sexual being, whether as a celibate or with a partner, must be an attempt to live out one of these two complementary principles; it can never be the attempt to live life without the masculine or the feminine. Any possibility of relationship with God requires acknowledgment and acceptance of who we are. It is not possible to love God or anyone else unless we begin by loving ourselves. And this includes our sexuality as the very secret intimacy of what we are. From earliest times, the great mystics saw sexuality as symptomatic of the self, and "sexual thoughts . . . as the barium-traces by which they mapped out the deepest and most private recesses of the will." Sexual manifestations were "the knot of unsurrendered privacy," and sexuality was for them "the ideogram of the unopened heart."[1]

Everything that is has two characteristics: inwardness and outwardness. *Intus, interior, intimus,* the Latin adjectives provide our words not only for the first of these, but also, in the comparative and superlative form, for "interior" and "intimate." What is innermost? Alienation means losing touch with that. The Latin verb *intimare* means to hint at, to publish, or to make known whatever is innermost. We don't, we can't, do this for many people. Sometimes we never achieve it at all. Our sexuality is what is most intimately ourselves. As sexual beings, we seek the deepest, most penetrating intimacy with another.

The sufferings of love are a privileged mode of understanding the most intimate core of our own being.

Without them it is difficult to see how we can ever reach the deep end of ourselves. Our solitude is even a dialectic between what is revealed to us through love, and what we are, what we become, after such a revelation, when we find ourselves alone again. If we never awaken this capacity, we live our lives at the shallow end. Of course it is dangerous to waken the sleeping lion, and there are problems that must not be underestimated. Addiction, for example, swamps and saps the energy of our more personal desire. It is a widespread panacea for anesthetizing this reality. Enslavement to sugar, nicotine, chemical substances, alcohol, work, and many kinds of sexual behavior, from masturbation to intercourse, afflicts a much larger percentage of the six billion people on the planet than we are inclined to believe.

There is a point of conflict that must be reached and passed if we are to get beyond our individuality and accede to personhood. Those who are supposedly celibate are sometimes those who not only have never passed beyond the point of conflict but have never reached it. And most efforts in our morality and spirituality seem directed toward keeping them on this side of the conflict. This is achieved by a very debilitating and castrating moral hygiene that simply prevents us from going right through to the far side of "happiness." "The only progress possible for such people might have to be accomplished in a humiliating breakdown of confidence, through being overwhelmed by some dramatically passionate experience."[2]

Our sexuality is the most private, the most intimate, the most idiosyncratic manifestation of who we are. It is as personal and as unique as our fingerprint. It tells us the secret of our deepest identity. It reveals part of the profoundest reality of what we are. It is at the very quick of our personhood. A loving relationship with another person expressed sexually can achieve what Peter Brown calls "the charis, the graciousness created by intercourse — that indefinable quality of mutual trust and affection gained through the pleasure of the bed itself,"[3] which is difficult to achieve without such privileged contact. Loving surrender skin to skin is a ritual that also makes humility easier. Humility is finding the outermost layer of our being, and being prepared to dwell at this frontier. Few incentives to do so are more effective than trusting, naked surrender to another person.

> But here no nymph comes naked to the youngest
>   shepherd,
> the fountain is deserted, the laurel will not grow;
>   the labyrinth is safe but endless, and broken
>   is Ariadne's thread,
>
> as deeper in these hands is grooved their fortune:
>   lucky
> were few, and it is possible that none was loved,
>   and what was god-like in this generation
>   was never to be born.
>
> *W. H. Auden*[4]

Commenting on this poem, Lilian Feder suggests that love, in the ancient myth, was the way out of the labyrinth.[5] But "the generation in which none were loved, however, never face the danger of the beast-man, but instead wander aimlessly in a labyrinth which they have not the courage to investigate or the incentive to leave."

It is essential to have Ariadne's thread securely fastened to the center of ourselves like a wick in a candle. This red thread of our lives, which is also the secret of our sexuality, has to be attached to the quick, before we start to pour the concrete that will form the mold into which we can securely settle ourselves inside our being, as a bone into its rightful socket. Otherwise we might set ourselves askew and become monuments to our own misalignment. Genuine human love is the most likely and appropriate compass to guide us to that nearly always dark and difficult place from which the secret of our life and our being emanates.

"Passion is by no means the fuller life which it seems to be in the dreams of adolescence, but is on the contrary a kind of naked and denuding intensity; verily, a bitter destitution, the impoverishment of a mind being emptied of all diversity, an obsession of the imagination by a single image."[6] This is true. We have seen it in the experience of infatuation. But passion is also an ascesis. The Greek word means "exercise, training, practice." So this naked and denuding intensity can have another more important effect.

This can be described if we take the image of light. In an ordinary light source, many excited atoms or molecules emit light independently in many different colors or wavelengths, diffusing the effect in every direction. In 1960 the discovery of "light amplification by stimulated emission of radiation" (the acronym is "laser') meant that if the atom can be stimulated to emit radiation that is in phase with the wave that stimulated it, and if the phenomenon can be multiplied sufficiently, then the resulting beam will be tremendously powerful because, instead of having rays that go off in all directions, it becomes one intensely concentrated, undiffused beam of "coherent" light. Such an instrument can be used to pulverize spaceships, drill holes in diamonds, or weld the retina of an eye, because of the precision, rapidity, and efficiency of the laser.[7]

My suggestion is that such a concentrated light makes up the reality of obsessive passion or infatuated love. These can thereby become reliable weapons in the task of splitting the atom of ourselves. This explosion is what transforms individuality into personhood. The single-minded and intense ray of such obsessive concentration gives us a direct road to the source from which it emanates. It leads us without decoy or delusion to the depth of our own life, to the quick of our innermost self. Of course it is dangerous. It can lead to despair, to addiction, to imprisonment. But if we can learn to keep the balance between our desire and the objects of our desire, this concentrated energy can help us both to dispel the myth of infatuated love and to discover the reality of who we are at our most intimate and personal. It is a concentrated light that is delicate enough to expose without damage the otherwise untouchable retina of the I. Such is the place we need to get to, and the person we need to meet, if we are to establish any real relationships and live a life that is authentically our own.

Sexual love can be the most powerful depth charge to the deepest reality of who we are, a reality that might otherwise be inaccessible. We are aiming at a moving target. Sexual love both moves us beyond what we are in our everyday existence and helps to create the person we become because of its demanding intensity. The kiss that makes the frog become a prince is not just cosmetic surgery; it is a personality transplant. It calls me into being; it makes me more than I ever was or ever would have been before it applied its shock treatment.

In other words, all of us have a journey to make before we become the person we were supposed to be. I am told that planet earth, as it is for us today, is the result of a balance between two conflicting forces. What is called "the curvature of space-time," the dimension in which we live and have our being, is the result of an unerringly accurate calculation in which the earth was launched. Had this curvature been larger, earth would have sunk into a black hole; had the curvature been smaller, earth would have exploded into multiple, lifeless fragments.

The two forces that maintain this balance, this knife-edge path between absorption and dissolution, are the original energy that caused its emergence in the first place, and its gravitational attraction to other planets. This tension holds it together and allows it to produce life. Why? Because "the resultant inner pressures combined with the earth's inner nuclear energy keep the earth in a state of balanced turbulence whence its continued transformation takes place. Because this balanced turbulence was not achieved in other planets they were unable to bring forth such living forms as emerged upon the earth." This means that the curvature is open enough to allow the earth to be creative and closed enough to allow its component parts to be integrated into and remain a coherent totality.[8]

Whether or not this is an entirely accurate account of the origin, life, and growth of planet earth is not within my competence to judge. I am using this account as a metaphor for our own life of desire. The source and the "gravitational attraction" of our desire is what gives us our particular blend of existence. It provides the turbulence that ensures that we are creative, that our life is one of constant transformation, able to produce life. The balance we have to achieve, the very precise curvature that we must maintain, is a difficult and narrow way between addiction and abnegation. Like the famous journey that Ulysses had to undertake on his Odyssey — which is something of a mythological blueprint for us who are the inheritors of the Greco-Roman world — between the deadly whirlpool of Charybdis, on the one hand, and Scylla, the sheer rock-faced cliff, on the other, our journey toward the correct alignment of our particular space-time curvature of desire has a similar tightrope walk between two possibilities of destruction. On the one hand, there is the possibility of being lived by our addictions, being swallowed up in the compulsive whirlpool of our neediness, dying for a drink, or whatever. On the other hand, there is the possibility of freezing ourselves into a rigid rock-face by cutting ourselves off from the source of our desire, and by so effectively insulating ourselves from any gravitational attraction that we become robots, mummies, walking corpses.

The rocky Scylla is a very understandable and elevated option. The other is far too murky, compromising, and fraught with danger. The balancing act of allowing both options to maintain a healthy tension in our lives is exposed to the ever-present possibility of falling, the constant threat of humiliation. No wonder that many cultures try to make us a little more solid, less volatile. This has been the history of education and spiritual development in western European culture, especially where we have been trying to create spiritual pastors and leaders.

It is a mistake to attribute the invention of such attitudes to Christianity itself.[9] Such a noble effort derives from much more ancient sources and, indeed, is shared by other cultures.

David Guterson, for example, gives us a model of a very similar kind of spiritual optic in Japanese culture.[10] Mrs. Shigemura is the spiritual guide to a young girl named Hatsue. "On Wednesday afternoons, she taught Hatsue the intricacies of the tea ceremony as well as calligraphy and scene painting. She showed her how to arrange flowers in a vase and how, for special occasions, to dust her face with rice powder." Hatsue is on her way to America, and so Mrs. Shigemura feels doubly motivated to teach her how to compose herself.

> Mrs. Shigemura taught her to seek union with the Greater Life and to imagine herself as a leaf on a great tree: the prospect of death in autumn, she said, was irrelevant next to its happy recognition of its participation in the life of the tree itself. In America, she said, there was fear of death; here life was separate from Being. A Japanese, on the other hand, must see that life embraces death, and when she feels the truth of this she will gain tranquillity.

Mrs. Shigemura tried to teach Hatsue how to sit without moving. She was certain that her protégé could not mature properly unless she learned to do this for extended periods, and living in America would make this difficult, because America was fraught with tension and unhappiness. At first Hatsue, who is only thirteen, was unable to sit still for even thirty seconds. As she eventually succeeds in quieting her body into stillness, she finds that it is her mind that cannot be kept still.

> But gradually her rebellion against tranquillity subsided. Mrs. Shigemura was pleased and claimed

that the turbulence of her ego was in the process of being overcome. She told Hatsue that her stillness would serve her well. She would experience harmony of being in the midst of the changes and unrest that life inevitably brings.

The outside appearance of tranquillity is superficial however. It is a lesson learned to satisfy a stern teacher. The young girl knows that this is not really her, not who she is at the deepest level of herself.

Hatsue feared, walking home over forest trails from Mrs. Shigemura's, that despite her training she was not becalmed. She dallied and sometimes sat under trees, searched for lady's slippers or white trilliums to pick, and contemplated her attraction to the world of illusions — her craving for existence and entertainment, for clothes, make-up, dances, movies. It seemed to her that in her external bearing she had succeeded only in deceiving Mrs. Shigemura; inwardly she knew her aspiration for worldly happiness was frighteningly irresistible. Yet the demand that she conceal this inner life was great, and by the time she entered high school she was expert at implying bodily a tranquillity that did not in fact inhabit her. In this way she developed a secret life that disturbed her and that she sought to cast off.

The danger of falling prey to the craving, needy side of ourselves causes certain groups to cauterize this side and to develop the tougher, more robust and harder side. Exaggerated promotion of either side to the exclusion of the other is unreal. Laurens van der Post talks about this unreality, using the imagery of two different continents inside ourselves, both of which have to be accommodated.

> Unreality starts in an incomplete awareness of ourselves; it starts in the elevation of a part of ourselves at the expense of the whole. Then out of this dark gorge which we have allowed to open up between the two halves of ourselves, out of this division between the Europe and the Africa in us, unreality rises up to overwhelm us.[11]

Whether or not we use the geographical imagery of continents, the mythological imagery of the Charybdis and Scylla, or the natural imagery of a whirlpool and a sheer rock face, we are pointing to the same psychological, emotional, and physical reality: the anarchy of passionate involvement, which can suck us into a vortex of addiction and dissolution, versus the hegemony of rational control, which can harden us into an impervious autonomy.

Overemphasis of the controlling, rational, rugged side of ourselves means filtering life through a process of detoxifying and insulating abstraction. This allows the Scylla syndrome to harden us into a suit of armor. The perversity of abstraction is that it bars your way just as it is pretending to let you in.[12] To the extent that intellectual knowledge — that is to say, abstract knowledge, separated from experience — precedes experience, it cannot have the flavor of life, but becomes for itself its own kind of experience, which is different, and which constitutes an almost insurmountable barrier to the possibility of plunging into waters that would be alive and life-giving. The Scylla syndrome emphasizes the soul as opposed to the body, the spirit as opposed to the flesh. Its disciples become souls who are trying to cure themselves of life. For these initiates it is as if life was not really life at all, but rather knowledge of rules and regulations *about* life. Such walking ghosts know what they should be living, and their life is meant to prove what they *know*, rather than be proof of what they have *lived*.

People who are involved in a process that separates them from their bodies cannot lose a life they have never had. Authors of their own relentless evaporation, they are always afraid of losing what they have never had. Their vigilance and fussy self-surveillance is unrelenting, and its inevitably strained sadness never turns into joy. Despite what they may say, their comportment is lifeless; its supervised quality guarantees listless inelegance, performance without vigor.

I think of a poem by Leopold Senghor, who believes there is a similar division between black people and white people:

New York! I say to you: New York let black blood
flow into your blood
That it may rub the rust from your steel joints, like
an oil of life,
That it may give to your bridges the bend of
buttocks and the suppleness of creepers.

New York is representative of the steel-girdered option,
which is that of the spirit pitted against the flesh. It is
the basic principle of all colonialism, the rule of the central power over the periphery, of the stronger over the
weaker, the one over the many. It was the basis of civilization as this was understood by nineteenth-century
colonial powers. Colonizers and missionaries went to
Africa to inculcate this option, to spread this particular gospel. "Let them come and see men and women
who know how to live, whose joy of life has not yet been
killed by those who claimed to teach them how to live!"
says Chinua Achebe, the Nigerian novelist. Brian Friel
had a similar intuition, which became his play *Dancing
at Lughnasa*. A missionary priest returns from Uganda to
teach the inhabitants of rural Ireland how to dance as
he had relearned to do in Africa. Friel's play ends:

> When I remember it, I think of it as dancing.
> Dancing with eyes half closed because to open
> them would break the spell. Dancing as if lan-
> guage had surrendered to movement — as if this
> ritual, this wordless ceremony, was now the way

to speak, to whisper private sacred things, to be in touch with some otherness.[13]

A story that tells the Scylla tale as another less daring way of being is about a young priest who fell in love with a woman. He went to a library and wrote her a long love-letter, pouring out his passion on the pages. He then climbed to the top shelves of the library, where there were books that were never used, ancient tomes. He took down one of these and put his letter somewhere in the center pages of one such book and replaced it on the forgotten shelf. He then left the library. This was meant to be some beautiful sacrifice of his desire, like a bottle of perfume opened in the desert. The story served to clarify my own thought and make me determined to allow no such abnegation to occur in my life. "Still full of sap, still green" one of the psalms says, meaning that we are meant to be prototypes of such greenness and vitality, embodying the full life, the way to more abundant vitality, promised by the Godman.

The alternative way to the daunting passage between the Scylla and the Charybdis involved another treacherous journey through the "Wandering Rocks." These wandering rocks must have been some kind of archipelago that gave sailors an optical illusion that the islands were floating and constantly crashing into each other. The most vivid description of these road hazards is given in Jason's search for the Golden Fleece. He sent a dove to show him the way. The dove chose its moment and flew through the clashing rocks. It got through, losing only the tip of its tail. Jason followed its "curvature in space" and passed through unscathed, except for some minor damage to the *Argo*'s stern.

The wandering rocks are something akin to the objects of desire. We have to take this route because, otherwise, we are in danger of losing ourselves in the softness of indulgence or the harshness of asceticism. I must follow the red thread of my own desire. But I have to go beyond it. I have to recognize the mirage that was leading me toward pastures new. Instead of chasing the wind and running after rainbows, I have to deconstruct the idol, disconnect the machinery that is automatically disgorging these clay pigeons for me to shoot, examine the nature of the dynamo within myself that is causing this displaced energy, and set about establishing appropriate relationships between myself as source of love and those around me, or beyond me, who can be reciprocating beneficiaries.

One of the people in the twentieth century most aware of these realities and most capable of expressing them was Rainer Maria Rilke, much of whose creative life was devoted to "questions of the ontology of the sexes, of what finally and at the deepest level the feminine is, of what being-human is, of what, most importantly, love is." His sensitive answers to these questions show that his "justly famed deep spirituality is rooted finally and forever in the earth, in the senses, in sex." He leads us convincingly towards "sacral love."

And the unusual conclusion of all his investigation into personal, sexual relationship is expressed in the maxim: "That each should stand guard over the solitude of the other."

A good marriage is one where each appoints the other guardian of this solitude. Togetherness is an impossibility, and wherever it seems to exist, it is a narrowing. It is a reciprocal agreement that robs either one or both parties of their fullest freedom and development. If we can accept that even between the closest human beings infinite distances continue to exist, then a healthy living side by side can grow. If couples succeed in loving the distance between them, this makes it possible for each to see the other as a complete entity and against a wide sky.

People who always insist on giving themselves, abandoning themselves, are harming genuine companionship: "for when a person abandons himself, he is no longer anything, and when two people both give themselves up in order to come close to each other, there is no longer any ground beneath them and their being together is a continual falling."

Young people who love each other fling themselves and don't notice what a lack of mutual esteem lies in this disordered giving of themselves; they notice it with astonishment and indignation when dissension arises from this disorder. And once there is disunity between them, the confusion grows with every day; neither of the two has anything unbroken, pure, and unspoiled about them any longer, and amid the disconsolateness of a break they try to hold fast to the semblance of their happiness. Alas, they are scarcely able to recall what they meant by happiness. In this uncertainty each becomes more and more unjust toward the other; they who wanted to do each other good are now handling one another in an imperious and intolerant manner, and in the struggle to get out of their state of confusion they commit the greatest fault that can happen to human relationships: they become impatient.[14]

Chapter Seven

BEYOND
THE PATHETIC

I T IS EASY TO SPEAK, easy to play with ideas. It is easy to say: "Listen to being — your own and everyone else's." That is an idea. Perhaps even a good idea. But it doesn't work. "I knew one fighter for an idea," Dostoevsky again, "who told me himself that when he was deprived of tobacco in prison, he was so distressed by this privation that he nearly went and betrayed his 'idea' just to get a little tobacco! And it is such a man who says: 'I am fighting for humanity'! How can a man give up his habits, where can such a slave go, if he is so used to satisfying his innumerable needs that he himself has created?"

It is one thing to say: "Be, don't have. Be free to desire and not a slave to need. To love means to let go. True life is humble obedience to being, our own and everyone else's. Listen all your life to the mystery of who you are. Play out your life in the key of desire, desire as the secret of your being." That is all nonsense when I am actually faced by the possibility of distraction, when addiction, in whatever guise, calls me.

It may be true that it is a beautiful and a noble thing to live one's life at this level, with arched wings and elegantly poised neck, a swan on a lake, but to most people it is uselessly boring and impossible stagnation. It is a form of exile or banishment from the bustling and hectic red and yellow world of desire, as I want to live it and be lived by it, the quick-fix world of ecstasy and exhaustion that sucks me in and wrings me out, and I love it. It is true that nothing lasts, that poignant moments of frustration or postcoital tristitia might prompt us toward celibacy, but such moments only add sauce to the slavery and make us yearn for an even more powerful and endearing tyrant to occupy our nervous energy. And so often the solution being proposed is some kind of understanding, a metaphysics, some sterile branch of philosophy! Shakespeare speaks our contempt in the words of Romeo, who hears that his punishment is banishment from Juliet and Verona:

> Yet "banished"? Hang up philosophy!
> Unless philosophy can make a Juliet,
> Displant a town, reverse a prince's doom,
> It helps not, it prevails not. Talk no more.

The overwhelming experience of humanity teaches us that, however tragic our situation is, however frustrating our desire may be, this is the only life we have, the only one of which we are capable. We cannot believe in banishment or exile. We cannot believe in life at a level of being where needs would hold no sway. And even if we did begin to believe it, experience again teaches us that we could never find within ourselves the power to achieve it, to reach these silent, secure, and unruffled depths. In the end, we are cripples proud of our crutches. We howl for mercy but dread the effective answer to our prayer.

The answer to these very real and natural misgivings is that we must go further than this, we must shift gears and move our desiring up a register, without thereby losing the essence of what it is, or of what we are. It is not a question of either/or, of choosing this world or the next world, of choosing God or creation, of being human or being divine. It is a question of all/and. What is being proposed in these chapters is not exclusion, denial, mortification, destruction of some particular element of what we are now, in order to develop some hybrid variation of ourselves, grafted onto the stem at a point above those areas that we intend to bypass or eliminate. The evolution that we can achieve will be a transformation and elevation of the whole human being to a level where the imperatives of biological reproduction will not be as pressing or overpowering, but where the vocation to love will be more specifically human, more personal, more total.

It is a question of becoming fully human. Our whimpering reluctance is understandable in the way that it is understandable not to want to get out of bed in the

morning or not to want to get into an airplane and fly.
Most children regret having to become adults; perhaps
caterpillars resent having to push themselves through becoming butterflies. But the point is this: We were made
to be persons and persons in love; anything less is dimin-
ishment, deprivation, abnegation. The word "person"
was invented by Judeo-Christianity to cope with the im-
mense reality people were discovering about themselves,
because they had been chosen as love objects by God.
And God came on earth to teach these same people
the meaning of the word "love." Love is that adhe-
sive and corrosive element that shackles us to the loved
one like prisoners chained together. It then eats back
into our interior reality, excavating spaces until then
unexplored, opening us out in ways unimagined, until
eventually we become the infinity that we are by virtue
of our personhood. Each one of us is an impenetrable,
unique, everlasting mystery. This wonder of our being,
this completeness of our personhood, which makes us
equal to every other person, is undiscovered potential
until developed in the darkroom of love.

And the use of the word "love" here is what we,
all of us, mean by love. It is our wonderfully romantic
and exciting notion of being *in* love, but it is this reality stretched to infinity, packed with ice, stitched with
salt, multiplied incrementally beyond everything we have
ever experienced or imagined. It is love everlasting.

And it happens between us, as well as between us
and God. Love between partners who allow the time,

the struggle, the patience, and the relentless persistence necessary to reveal to one another the height and the depth, the length and the breadth of their own mysterious personhood, is the fruit and the fulfillment of their original infatuation, their earliest intuition of each other.

Couples who stay together do not become different people, nor does their exciting connection need to change from being an adolescent explosion of infatuated desire to a dull complacent cohabitation resulting from a mixture of laziness and habit. Romeo and Juliet do not have to become Darby and Joan, in some butterfly-back-to-caterpillar trajectory. Love makes both become persons. Octavio Paz calls love the point of intersection between desire and reality: "Love reveals reality to desire." Love is the magic middle term "creating the transition from the erotic object to the beloved person." Love makes the person you were originally infatuated with into a real human being, if you can wait around long enough, and weather the storms and the shocks that such a heady transformation process of necessity entails. Sometimes this persistence can rely upon the enduring energy of attraction; if this wears out, it may be necessary to switch gears to the sheer determination of willpower; and if this also expires, there is always the automatic pilot of what Bridget Riley in another context describes as "bloody obstinacy."

If allowed the time, love does change us from being possessive and grasping individuals to becoming open and radiating centers of generosity. If we don't allow it to do that to us, if we remain in the shape and gesture of a claw, we are led to murder because of fear, because of jealousy, because of mistrust. Shakespeare is again the master portrait painter who shows us to ourselves in this guise. His Othello is infatuated love that will not move forward.

The drama takes place within the area of the bedchamber, as opposed to the public domain, the battlefield, where the mighty Moor is champion. Othello, like each one of us, is made up of two parts, two places: one a public, political, performer's pedestal, the other a secret sexual sanctuary; the first is a battlefield, the second a bedchamber. Shakespeare further defines the two places geographically as Venice and Cyprus. In the first place Othello is a soldier, a leader; in the second he is a frightened, naked animal. The drama unfolds in the study of the relationship between the two parts of himself. Neglect of the second must always lead to the downfall of the first, even though it may be the prime motivation for success in the first instance. Downfall in war stems from essential insecurity, a fear that in himself he is unacceptable and can secure his public standing only by rendering himself indispensable. He would never have allowed anyone into that private place behind the public persona had Desdemona not attracted him sufficiently to let her in. She alone broke through the barriers and visited the shivering creature in the inner cell; she traveled with him to Cyprus and entered the stormy zone of unbridled, uncontrollable love.

Cyprus is introduced with storms raging around its shores. At that time it was the furthermost outpost of the Venetian empire and in constant danger of being invaded by Turks. It represents the opposite pole to Venice, portrayed in the play's first act as a world of high civilization, ordered government, social sophistication, and great wealth, around which the sea has been domesticated and harnessed into canals and channels supporting the civilization they irrigate and enhance.

Why does Othello make this dangerous journey on the night of his wedding to such a barren, storm-tossed outpost of civilization? Ostensibly, the reason is to protect the state against invasion; his bride travels with him because she has been ostracized by her own family and has nowhere else to go. Her decision to marry him has condemned her to solitary confinement on his island. As they arrive through the storms, we discover that the original purpose of their journey has been removed: "News, friends, our wars are done, the Turks are drowned." As simple as that — the battle is over. But this just clears the stage for the real battle. On this island, in this secret, private place, we are all old, dark, frightened savages who cannot believe we are loved. And it is this cowering, frightened predisposition in the inner place that allows the Iago in each of us to exploit us and give birth to the tragedy. This tragedy is the destruction, through jealousy, of the most precious gift any human being can receive. "Trifles light as air, are to the jealous confirmation strong as proofs of holy writ," and are the basis of our accusations against our partner, with, of course, no consultation whatsoever. Such a tragedy can come only from a source totally corrupted — that second place, the bedchamber, Cyprus, where we find ourselves deformed, starving, terrified, inarticulate, self-loathing creatures.

Once the accusation is made and the sentence has been passed, the public persona takes over. The general, the soldier, the judge, the high priest all prepare to execute the traitor who has deserted. The place is dark, and it is night. He utters a prayer over Desdemona and kisses her. He asks her to admit her crimes and, when she refuses, he kills her. This is a terrible place, the inner sanctuary, where any creature who dares to enter has to die. The one inside is so loathsome to himself that he has to project this feeling onto the other and, despite every demonstration and protest to the contrary, must persist in believing that no one can love him. The play is a dramatization of this inner place; it describes "the time, the place, the torture." Emilia, Desdemona's maid, identifies Othello's real unworthiness to be her mistress's husband — not his age, his class, or his ethnicity, but his incapacity to believe in the gift that was their love.

It is not always necessary to kill the one you love. There is another way of loving. But it is the same love in a purified form. Sexual passion "implies a courageous delivery of the self to a desired union with the ideal other in the face of unavoidable dangers." It does take us to the bedchamber after the stormy voyage to Cyprus. Otto Kernberg, an experienced professor of psychiatry and psychoanalysis, holds, on the basis of his evaluation of couples in longstanding relationships, that passionate love endures for some couples during many years of life together, and that sexual passion should not be equated with an ecstatic mood of adolescence. "It constitutes a permanent feature of love relations" and "has the function of providing intensity, consolidation, and renovation to love relations throughout life." He thinks that "clinical evidence clearly indicates how intimately sexual excitement and enjoyment are linked to the quality of a couple's total relationship."[1]

Passionate infatuation can and does begin with a distortion of the loved object and a projection of unconscious data onto a falsified identity. Love can transform this passion, however, without lessening its intensity, into a genuine relationship with another person. Negotiating the storms and the minefields that may always hamper communication, two people can still reach each other in love. We are, at the deepest level, relational beings. And the basic meaning of love consists in learning to recognize the absolute significance, the inalienable identity, and the sovereign autonomy of another personality.

Love as passionate infatuation helps us to transcend our egoistic selves by breaking down the limits of selfhood. But it leads only to an *égoïsme à deux*, a combined selfishness, unless the dawn of a new kind of loving opens up vaster horizons. We are born as *individuals*; we become *persons* by opening up to love. We achieve such personhood by breaking down the walls of individuality, opening out the armor that surrounds us like a shell, and expanding into the space between us and other people. This space between — some refer to this as potential space, because it does not have to be appropriated, and can remain uninhabited — is beyond our natural boundaries. We stretch into it like snails emerging with highly sensitive antennae from our shells. If our experience of reaching out is hostile, if we feel acid being poured on us when we first reach out, our instinctive reaction is to recoil and withdraw within the protected boundaries of our shell. The great enemy of such important expansion into the relational realm is fear.

Even physiologically, fear causes us to retire from this outer realm into the depths of ourselves. We grow pale or faint because our energy, our bodily fluids, drain from the skin back into the center. When, on the other hand, we meet someone we really want to meet, everything rushes to the edges of our skin in a movement outward toward that person. The blood rushes to our cheeks, and we are literally flushed with excitement. But even beyond that skin, there is a space that we can invade, and this occupation of the zone of otherness is what makes us a person. Around the walled castle of our individuality, we must develop the circumambient passage into the space beyond us. These extensions to ourselves, these bridges and channels, windows and passages, are what give us the structure, the scaffolding of care or concern. Care cultivates personhood.

This development into the full scope of our societal ambience requires a release from the tentacles of individuality. Among the most difficult of these knots to untie is what Martin Heidegger calls "the addiction to becoming 'lived' by the world and not to be rooted out."[2] Passivity, inertia, depression, moodiness, sulkiness, sickness, and helplessness all prevent that sinking back into the primal element, the summoning up of those juices from the marrow that would transform our being into the open form of "care" and turn relatedness into "sympathy." Rainer Maria Rilke calls this a "turning." Some religions call it a "conversion."

In a poem called "Turning," Rilke quotes Kassner's aphorism that "the way from intensity to greatness leads through sacrifice." Rilke describes a hard kind of gazing, a wrestler's look, which becomes "a calm perception at evening" into which animals can trustfully enter and lions can stare "as into incomprehensible freedom." But the real "turning" is from the eyes of the head to those of the heart:

> Work of sight is achieved,
> now for some heart-work
> on all those images, prisoned within you; for you
> overcame them, but do not know them as yet.
> Behold, O man within, the maiden within you! —
> creature wrung from a thousand natures, creature
> only outwrung, but never,
> as yet, belov'd.[3]

This poem expresses how Rilke made such a change in himself. "And I, who still do nothing but crave. — Begin over again." The poem was written between June 18 and 20, 1914. He sent it immediately to Lou Andreas-Salome: "Lou, dear, there's a strange poem, written this morning, which I'm sending you right away, because I involuntarily called it "Turning," since it portrays the turning that will certainly have to come if I am to live." He had commented on an earlier version of the poem: "May this gazing out of myself, which consumes me to emptiness, be rid of through a loving preoccupation with interior fullness." What he meant by "this gazing out of myself" is made explicit in a previous letter to Lou (October 1913):

> Will you believe me, when I tell you that the sight of a woman who passed me in a quiet street in Rouen so disturbed me, that thereafter I could see almost nothing, concentrate on nothing?...I'm alarmed when I think of the way I've been living out of myself, as though always standing at a telescope, ascribing to every woman who approached a bliss that could certainly never have been discovered in one of them.

A new kind of opening out of ourselves — so that we no longer suck everything into the vacuum of our own possessive neediness, but become smooth-surfaced vessels into which and out of which love can pour freely and generously — this is a worthwhile, though hard-won, accomplishment. It means flattening out our hands and beating them into open surfaces. Depending on how grasping or clenched our fingers happen to be, the extent to which we have used them as claws or as tentacles, will dictate the amount of time and effort necessary to change their instinctual gestures and shape. But it can be done, and it must be done if we wish to arrive at the fullness of personhood.

The notion that we are born to be inescapably selfish, that our instincts and habits are too deeply ingrained to be eradicated, that we are biologically determined victims of a precoded system that dictates our behavioral responses and predetermines fated enslavement to those who turn us on, is belied by recent scientific research. What is called the "constructionist view" of evolution suggests that we are not only capable of changing ourselves and our environment, but that we are biologically constructed to do so. Far from being predetermined either by our environment or our genes, we are provided with an adaptive plasticity that awaits our decisive action before it forms us into the eventual shape we choose to become. Obviously lions produce lions in our kind of world, and human beings produce human beings. But not every lion is the same, and human beings are not only different but are capable of becoming whatever kind of human being they choose to become.

In this context, we are not hardwired by our hormones toward addictive infatuation. At the level of breathing, sneezing, and swallowing, our reactions are genetically determined, but "at higher levels, where learning occurs, an entirely new principle of organization comes into being. These areas are uncommitted at birth, and their development depends on the particularities of life experience: they assume a function in the course of life."[4] In other words, the shape of who we are as human beings emerges under the influence of what we believe, what we want, and what we experience. "At every moment every species is in the process of creating and re-creating, both beneficially and detrimentally, its own conditions of existence, its own environment."[5]

The feeling of love is a stimulus suggesting to us that we can and must re-create ourselves as human beings geared toward the meaning it heralds. Every act of loving is making us more capable of life as lovers. Without love we can create ourselves into monsters, into towers of strength, bastions of power, impregnable fortresses. Love is what prevents development from being depersonalized. It is the compelling reminder of what is most intimate, most heartwarming, most important. Evolution occurs in the direction toward which humanity strains. Limbs drop off as they become redundant, others sprout or change shape and texture, to adjust to the task, the environment, the purpose. Scales become skin; fins become wings. Our hands become claws, fingers, fists, or delicate wings, depending upon how we decide to touch.

If genuine love is allowed to transform our desire, our whole bodies become radiating centers of energy, with newly developed centrifugal structures of generosity, allowing our whole being to express concern. The word "concern" is synonymous with compassion, care, charity, and sympathy, depending upon the tradition we have been brought up with. "Care" is the word selected by Heidegger, for instance; "sympathy" is Thomas Mann's word.

> Sympathy, a rather tame word for so profound an emotion. . . . For sympathy is a meeting of life and death; true sympathy exists only where the feeling for the one balances the feeling for the other. Feeling for death by itself makes for rigidity and gloom; feeling for life by itself, for flat mediocrity and dull-wittedness. Wit and sympathy can arise only where veneration for death is moderated, has, so to speak, the chill taken off by friendliness to life; while life, on the other hand, acquires depth and poignancy.[6]

"Concern" emphasizes the discernment and discretion necessary when installing a free distribution system for any kind of energy [*com* = with + *cernere*, to sift]. All these words, if correctly understood, are saying the same thing, which is love. Teilhard de Chardin hopes that the exponential increase of humanity, the tightening of the human mass, which necessarily throws us on top of one another, will force us to "enter the powerful, still unknown field of our basic affinities. In other words, that attraction will one day be born of enforced nearness." We have recently passed the six billion mark in the world's population. If we continue at the rate we're going, there will be at least twice that number by the end of this century. The fact that we are all going to be crushed together in the subway, however, is not going to produce intimacy of its own accord. Teilhard de Chardin believes "in the hidden existence and eventual release of forces of attraction between people which are as powerful in their own way as nuclear energy appears to be, at the other end of the spectrum of complexity."[7]

But love is as yet only in its infancy. Vladimir Soloviev, the Russian mystic and philosopher, suggests that love in its present form is no more than a feeling. Just as before the evolution of rational consciousness, reason in the animal kingdom was no more than a vague striving toward the organ of the brain, so love exists only as a rudimentary token of what it could be, if we were to live it in a way that forced us to make a similar breakthrough. The difference is that rational consciousness emerged in humankind without our conscious involvement, whereas the similar breakthrough in the realm of love would have to happen in us and through us. It could not happen in spite of us.

> The entire complex of interhuman and intercosmic relations will become charged with an immediacy, an intimacy and a realism such as has long been dreamed of and apprehended by certain spirits particularly endowed with the "sense of the universal,"

but which has never yet been collectively applied. And it is in the depths and by the grace of this new inward sphere, the attribute of planetized life, that an event seems possible which has hitherto been incapable of realization: I mean the pervasion of the human mass by the power of sympathy. It may in part be passive sympathy, a communication of mind and spirit that will make the phenomenon of telepathy, still sporadic and haphazard, both general and normal. But above all it will be a state of active sympathy in which each separate human element, breaking out of its insulated state under the impulse of the high tensions generated in the Noosphere, will emerge into a field of prodigious affinities.... For if the power of attraction between simple atoms is so great, what may we not expect if similar bonds are contracted between human molecules?[8]

Our task is to strive in the direction of love as "concern" and as radiating outward energy, in such a way and to such an extent that this becomes the intentionality and the structure of our own being. We can become embodied organisms of love. This in turn would communicate itself to others, making it easier for them to move into the same space of otherness until, eventually, such specimens of humanity would become the exemplary forms toward which the evolutionary appetite would aspire. Eventually habit and effort would become inscribed, and we would begin to take this shape and structure. Human beings would then be born to love. This would establish a very different kind of universe, one that did justice to the word "uni-verse," meaning all of us turned toward each other, turned into one.

Christianity would claim to have produced a number of pioneers leading us in the direction of such an evolution toward love. Francis of Assisi is the most obvious. His stigmata, meaning the appearance of the five wounds of Christ in his body, symbolize the quality and the kind of transformation that must take place to transform the human body into a dynamo of love. The pentagram, or sign of the five wounds, spells out the areas and the extent to which we have to be pinned down in our natural energy and movement. The dark currents of our natural energy, our human will, make us want to be great, want to take and to keep, to move forward at the expense of others and appropriate what belongs to others. The crucifixion, the wounding, the nailing down of our two hands, our two feet, and our hearts, symbolizes the way to puncture, to open up these sources of energy and movement, allowing the energy of God to flow through them. In the Christian dispensation, the vow of poverty pins down our two hands and trains them not to grasp or to keep; the vow of chastity prevents the natural feet of the hunter from setting traps and moving in on others in a predatory way; the vow of obedience to God tempers our desire for greatness and our will to power. The stigma is a sketch design of what our limbs and organs might become in the future if we followed this lead and practiced these virtues.

Such transformation would leave our sexuality and our desire intact. It would make them capable of the deepest personal love. Not simply to allow us to love one another, but so that "in the end," as Rilke says, "we shall have been marvelously prepared for divine relationship."

Chapter Eight

INTIMACY WITH GOD

Where have you hidden,
Beloved, and left me yearning?
You fled like the stag
after wounding me;
I went out calling you, and you were gone.
. . . .
All who are free
tell me a thousand graceful things of you.
. . . .
With flowers and emeralds
chosen on cool mornings
we shall weave garlands
flowering in your love,
and bound with one hair of mine.
You considered
that one hair fluttering at my neck;
you gazed at it upon my neck
and it captivated you;
and one of my eyes wounded you.

. . . .

Let us rejoice, Beloved,
and let us go forth to behold ourselves in your beauty,
to the mountain and to the hill,
to where the pure water flows,
and further, deep into the thicket.

And then we will go on
to the high caverns in the rock
which are so well concealed;
there we shall enter
and taste the fresh juice of the pomegranates.[1]

I AGREE WITH EVELYN UNDERHILL that the "whole business and method of mysticism is love."[2] This particular kind of love is love of God. It is the human way of realizing such love, achieving the most satisfactory union with God. This means that we remain fundamentally who and what we are. We love with the heart, the humanity, the embodied person that we are. We can do whatever is necessary to achieve this goal: We can deny ourselves, channel our emotions, restrict our enthusiasm, discipline and train our bodily impulses, if we believe that any or all of these are necessary. We cannot disown our incarnate being, however. We love whatever we love, animal, human, and divine, with and through the body, which is ourselves. Any relationship with God that would require the destruction of this incarnate being would amount to blasphemy. It would foist upon God an image of himself as genocidal monster requiring the ethnic cleansing of his creature before it becomes acceptable. Unless mystical union with God is total and inclusive, preserving and incorporating the comprehensive reality of myself, it is not a relationship of love between God and myself.

From the human point of view, such a relationship cannot be dependent upon any external or cultural factor. No qualification of race or creed is prerequisite. Each unique human person can be approached and can approach without intermediary of any kind. "The Spirit blows where it will." Church authority can authenticate such experience, or it can repudiate it; but it can neither guarantee nor monopolize it. Mysticism is possible and has been possible between God and unique individuals from every tribe, tongue, people, and nation, since Adam and Eve walked with God in the cool of the evening. Teresa of Avila says that "contemplative prayer is nothing else than a close sharing between friends."

There is no guaranteed method or teachable way of achieving such a relationship. Each person has to do whatever is necessary to make this contact. If, as we are told, there are now six billion people alive on this planet, then there are no fewer than six billion possible ways of communicating with God.

Although the methods and the ways are several and varied, the thing to be done, the one thing necessary, is always the same. T. S. Eliot puts it succinctly:

Quick now, here, now, always —
A condition of complete simplicity
(Costing not less than everything).[3]

This one thing necessary can be described as a going down to the deepest level of yourself, stripping yourself naked, complete abandonment to God, self-surrender — all of which are metaphors, ways of describing the gift of self and the ecstasy of communion between lovers. Nakedness, vulnerability, descent to the depths, seem to approximate the way to the kind of loving that mysticism is. The danger about describing what we do and prescribing exercises that might help is that we risk substituting another activity, however sublime and worthwhile in itself, for the one thing necessary. Most recommended teaching about prayer and purification ranges from the ludicrous to the inadequate. No one should presume to teach another the path to union with God. All one can do is point the way and affirm the possibility. There are no matchmakers, no go-betweens, no pimps. There can be no intermediary, no third term, either as teacher or as technique, between God and the individual person at this level.

What has to be done has to be done by me. And it is easy to say it. It amounts to my reaching the Point Zero of my being. In such a place there is no deceiving myself. This is such an intimate and ownmost part of myself that arrival there, and what happens there, are recorded at the quick in such a way that they are undeniable. They become me. The place in itself has nothing essentially religious about it. It can be reached by different techniques and for many purposes. It is the perimeter of our being, the edge of ourselves — the space where we can meet God.

Terribilis est locus iste (this is a terrible place). Most who have been there and who have looked over this cliff find it terrifying or, at least, awe-inspiring. We are afraid of going there, and even more afraid of remaining there. As in the case of all love, however, the decision to make this rendezvous for the purpose of meeting a specific lover transforms the void. The meeting itself is occasioned, furnished, and marked by the natures of those who have chosen to connect.

Theologically speaking, in the Christian tradition, this is the mystery of *kenosis,* the Greek word for self-emptying. In the case of the Man-God, Jesus Christ, there was a double *kenosis.* He emptied himself of his Godhead so that he could become a person in our world. His life on earth was a further self-emptying of that nature (ours) which he had assumed, right to the Point Zero, the draining of the last drop on the cross, where the ultimate fusion occurred and the explosion of resurrection into a new kind of being, a new kind of loving, was effected.

Our direction, our movement, are similar to this second kind of *kenosis.* We empty ourselves until we reach that same Point Zero of our humanity, the very last skin between us and the abyss of nothingness, beyond which is the absolute otherness of God. When we reach that source of ourselves, that original point, that openness to the void at the last extreme of what we are, we find there a bridge that has been erected by, with, and through the person of Jesus Christ. He is the *pontifex,* the bridge-builder. The bridge is one that moves out over the abyss from two opposite sides and joins in the middle without actually merging or being soldered together. It meets but leaves a tantalizingly unnoticeable gap between each of the two sections. It is possible to meet on the bridge, but the two sides yet remain irretrievably rooted in the banks of their respective foundations, never achieving the merger at the center that might take some of the strain. The bridgeable gap between the two outstretched arms is maintained by a tension of engineering that allows both to remain forever always on the point of meeting. It is the place prepared for us since the beginning of time. St. Paul expresses it enigmatically in a pre-position (almost a dis-position), *"en" Christo* ("in" Christ). This tiny word represents the link, the space, forged through the person of Christ, in his divinity, for all time, and in his humanity at one specific historical moment. It signifies the stainless steel, tension-filled, parallel interface, bridging the gap without eliminating it, allowing availability, without access, from either side of the divide.

There is no necessity for us to be aware of the theological infrastructure put in place by divine engineering, not just since Jesus Christ came on earth, but, as St. Paul says, from the beginning of time. This ingenious salvage operation, constantly being implemented by the Trinity, has been made available in blueprint to those who have the privilege of initiation to the mysteries of Christianity as a religion. For the rest of humankind, even those who have never heard of Jesus Christ, the delicate infrastructure remains in place. It is possible for anyone to reach the outer limits, the cliffside, starting from whatever geographical or historical point happens to be their station of departure. They can then walk that bridge without either knowing what it is, or how it came to be. In technical theological terms, this is what is meant by saying that the achievement of hypostatic union is an ontological reality for all time.

So what prevents us from finding and using this bridge? Many, many things. Fear, guilt, ignorance, a sense of inferiority, unworthiness, uncleanness; these and other mists and fogs that pervade our being make it difficult for us to love or be loved. Especially when the lover is all-holy, all-pure, and all-powerful.

Freedom is what we need. Freedom from fear, freedom to love. Two things seem to be essential as preliminaries to any kind of relationship with God. The first is best expressed in the words "nakedness," "openness," vulnerability — whatever allows us to be there in his presence in the full stark reality of what we are. The second is whatever allows us to love and accept this reality in its every aspect and to trust that God also finds it lovable and acceptable to him. Both are summed up in a correct understanding of "humility."

Humility is neither a psychological attitude nor an ethical posture; it is an ontological level, a place we reach as ground of our being (*humus* in Latin means ground). As natures, God and I are irretrievably separated, incomparably other. It is only by the *kenosis*, whereby we as persons empty ourselves of our natures, that we reach that edge, the limit of our nature, and can relate to each other, can touch each other. The bridge built by, in, and through Christ achieved unity without diluting the integrity, or undermining the identity, of either nature on each side of the bridge. This means that, as human beings, we are saved in Christ both by our unity with God and by our separation from God. *Sozein*, the Greek word for being saved and the key word in the Council of Chalcedon, which defined the precise way in which this salvation occurred, means that our salvation in Christ was as much a saving of our nature *from* God as it was redemption by God. If the great divide between us is not scrupulously maintained, we would lose our identity and become absorbed into God.

Humility is the ground of our being, the last skin separating us from nothingness. Here we can open ourselves toward infinity. We exist from here as persons in a way that is beyond our nature. We can make our exodus from the limited being-toward-death of our human nature and pass over to a new form of existence in communion with God. This is the reality of resurrection. We shuffle off this mortal coil and move from the chrysalis of individual existence to the expansive flow of life with the persons of the Trinity, much as the butterfly does from its previous existence in a cocoon.

This is also why Christ must always leave us in his earthly body and separate himself from us, before this leap, this ascension to another level of existence is possible. Christ is that Point Zero, that bridge, that humility, which allows us access. But "Christ is nothing," Kierkegaard reminds us. "Never forget that, Christianity!"

Zero plus zero equals zero. At this level of being all is equal. This is by far the most important realization for us in our relationship with God. Unless we establish this equality between ourselves and God as lover, no real love relationship is possible.

And it is a difficult obstacle for most. We can misunderstand, sometimes to the point of outrage, what I am trying to explain here. When I propose equality with God as an essential prerequisite for a relationship of love, I am not suggesting some satanic urge to put ourselves at the same level, to identify ourselves with God. By nature God is infinite, all-powerful, and eternal; we are finite, powerless, and time-bound. There is no comparison and certainly no equality between God and us at this level of nature, of creation, of power.

The equality that is possible and necessary comes at the level of relationship, communion, love. Love is not possible without such equality between partners. It is the great mystery of God that he created us free to love or not to love. God did not want this love to be given to him out of necessity, compulsion, or fear. He wanted it to be a free gift. At this level of loving, every person is equal; every person is reduced to nothing; all people empty themselves of their nature, their power, their possessions; every person is weak, vulnerable, and naked. All of which applies to God as much as it applies to any other person. Both Old and New Testaments should be sufficient proof of this from God's point of view, but it is a shocking, even scandalous reality, which we prefer to forget or to condemn.

This is not just a clever equation creating an optical illusion of God reduced to our size. This is a reality that each of us knows all too well, even from our own meager experience of what it means to really love. Who has never tried to persuade persons who are younger or who regard themselves as inferior to love us as an equal? It could even be a child, your own child: "Be my friend, see yourself as my equal." But those individuals cannot get over their conviction that they are unworthy, beneath us, in another category or class altogether. It doesn't matter how much we try to plead or persuade that we are the same as them, persons without anything except open and empty hands: They cannot see it and we cannot convince them of it. This is the story of God's relationship with his chosen people and with each one of us.

But nothing less than this is the stark naked reality of pure relationship in love. If it has another agenda, if it

has business, political, territorial, or even theological in-
terests, it is no longer love at this level of the naked wires
of pure energy, and it moves into the area of inequality.

To relate to God in love, we have to be fully aware and
confident that he loves us, needs us, and hungers for our
love. We have to trust that he is always there, and that
any distance between us can be obliterated by our per-
sistent, obstinate presence. We have to trust and, at the
same time, patiently adjust ourselves to the unnatural
task of addressing ourselves to a lover who is deprived
of all the normal means we use to express and communicate our heart's desire. Our problem at this level is
perhaps analogously expressed by Henry Higgins when
he understands the difference between his way of loving
and Eliza Doolittle's and retorts in exasperation: "What
you call love is a thick pair of lips to kiss you with and a
thick pair of boots to kick you with."

Why is sexuality so connected with mysticism? From
the book of Genesis in the Bible to the ecclesiology of
St. Paul, this has been the preferred metaphor used to
explain God's relationship with us and Christ's relationship with his church. Unless we accept, understand, and
honor the conjugal relationship between a man and a
woman, we cannot understand the relationship between
God and his creation, between Christ and the church:
"In His own image he created them, male and female He
created them." Mysticism has always been described in
such terms.

The Song of Songs is erotic love poetry. Many mystics have been attracted to this work as an expression of what they understand about their relationship with God as lover. Origen, Bernard of Clairvaux, Meister Eckhart, John of the Cross have all written or preached about it. We are told by some that they are understanding the text in a different nonphysical way. I cannot accept that they are talking about anything different from the way we fall in love with the only heart we have for loving. The aspect of human relationship that makes mystical experience more tangibly understandable is coital sexual union. The time of orgasm when both partners are in ecstasy is the kind of transport that mystics describe as union with the divine. I am aware of the difficulties and the ambiguities that such language and such comparisons involve. These must not allow us, however, to deny the fundamental reality and sameness of what we are trying to describe.

Of course we are aware that our relationship with God is not the same as a sexual relationship with another human being. Yet what we are trying to achieve is the same kind of intensity of relationship between persons.

Blind, deaf, and dumb, Hellen Keller shows how the whole explosion of human communication can happen through the one sense of touch. Love is possible between a lover and the beloved who is paralyzed and enclosed in an iron lung. Analogously, love of God is possible for us by total orientation of every particle of our being, including our sexuality, toward God as object of our love. This does not mean that we can prescribe either what should happen or what will happen. We hold ourselves out to the darkness with trust and energetic love. We know that the darkness is not such because God is hiding or withdrawn or playing some game; it is the way he is in relation to what we are. All our normal ways of loving, of expressing love, must shrivel, and we are left with the palpitating core. Attuning to the difference, acclimating to the emptiness, adjusting our receivers to the unde-tectable refinement of his presence, registered on our radar screens as blankness and in our sound recorders as silence, is kissing the dark.

Instead of losing interest or running away in panic, if we can allow this presence to seep through the sur-face of frustrated senses and sink to the person who is me at the core of myself, it gets there with a textureless infiltration of love. At the deepest level of personhood, despite the lack of adequate or even primitive means of communication, there is a person-to-person compatibil-ity, if I can register its impact at a depth I do not usually acknowledge. Eventually such contact excavates within us its own acoustic chamber; it widens us, opens us, and makes us detectably compatible. Invaded by immensity, we eventually expand to this horizon.

There have been many examples of such mystical union in every religious tradition. John of the Cross (1542–91), the Spanish Carmelite, is one of the most striking because of his poetic gift, which allowed him to communicate his experience of God so effectively. He sees the beloved "in nakedness of spirit." In his search and in his writings he had no other light or guide than the one that burned in his heart. His life of "burning love" flowed into a poetry that even he could not fully understand or explain. He says that in the beginning we are hardly aware of the refined, scarcely detectable, subtle, and silent breathing of divine love. But he assures us: "If a person is seeking his God, his beloved is seeking him much more." I will concentrate here on two texts of his that emphasize the necessity for equality between God and ourselves in the refined and delicately textured cobweb of God's kind of loving, to which we eventually become attached:

> This breathing of the air is an ability. . . . By his divine breath-like spiration, the Holy Spirit elevates the soul sublimely and informs her and makes her capable of breathing God in the same spiration of love that the Father breathes in the Son and the Son in the Father. This spiration of love is the Holy Spirit himself. . . . And this kind of spiration . . . is so sublime, delicate and deep a delight that a mortal tongue finds it indescribable. . . . In the transformation that the soul possesses in this life, the same spiration passes from God to the soul and from the soul to God with notable frequency and blissful love, although not in the open and manifest degree proper to the next life. . . . One should not think

it impossible that the soul be capable of so sublime an activity as this breathing in God through
participation as God breathes in her.[4]

The abyss between the soul and God must remain as
a skin or dividing line. And yet the communion between
them is so possible that the mystics often use the metaphor of a kiss to suggest the most intimate communion
between lips that remain forever contained within their
own circumference and yet are capable of exchanging the
most blissful love. "I have become lost in his mouth,"
one of the beguines says of Christ. John of the Cross
comments on his own use of such imagery:

> This is what the bride wanted to say in the Song
> of Songs: Who will give you to me for my brother,
> nursed at the breasts of my mother, that I may
> find you alone outside and kiss you, and no one
> despise me?
> This kiss is the union of which we speak, in
> which the soul is made equal with God through
> love. Because of this desire she asks who will give
> her the Beloved as her brother (which would both
> signify equality and produce it).[5]

This daring statement about equality with God almost
had these writings banned and this passage altered, because it was feared that the Spanish Inquisition might
condemn John's works out of hand.

The experience of resurrected love, of love that is nothing less than divine, comes across to the human person as something dark, dangerous, and difficult. It depends upon my own state of mind as to whether certain conditions, circumstances, and atmospheres are described by me as agony or ecstasy, as pleasure or pain, as boredom or expectation.

Is the relationship between Cathy and Heathcliff in *Wuthering Heights* to be called "love" or "brutal abuse"? The Marquis de Sade has taught us to be careful when we say, "I love you," having given his name to a version of it not easily distinguishable from cruelty. So when we "experience" the "love" of God, will we regard this as a burdensome or a beautiful experience? This will depend very largely upon our expectations, our cultural baggage. Most of us have already written the script for this movie and, of course, we are bored to tears and frustrated when nothing happens as we had imagined.

My own experience of God's presence is of some very timid and painfully sensitive aristocrat who disappears when the slightest movement is made in his direction, who waits and watches with tremulous delight and eager attention at the other side of a hedge. But any attempt to acknowledge his presence or to include him in our preoccupation makes him start and disappear. Anxiously friendly, curious but terrified, like wild deer you surprise in a wood. Shy to the point of agony, overwhelmed by fear of disturbing or of frightening. The Elephant Man.

The Hunchback of Notre Dame. Haunted by the in-
evitability of being kept at arm's length as an outsized
monstrosity, with a horror of imposing himself and discovering his presence to be unbearable to us. And yet,
there is this helpless, almost pathetic plea for acknowledgment. Nothing more than an understated gesture,
a signal in the night. And the contact that eventually builds up proves to be the most enduring, the most
exciting, the most worthwhile, even though always con-
ducted at his tempo, in this idiom, with almost painful
minimalism and restraint.

Rainer Maria Rilke says a similar thing in one of his
letters:

> Russia opened out for me and gave me the brother-
> liness and darkness of God, in whom alone there is
> fellowship. That is how I named him then, the God
> who has dawned upon me, and I lived long in the
> antechamber of his name, on my knees. . . . Now,
> you would hardly ever hear me name him, there
> is an indescribable discretion between us, and
> where closeness and penetration once were, new
> distances stretch out. . . . The tangible slips away,
> changes; instead of possession one learns the rel-
> ativity of things, and there arises a namelessness
> that must begin again with God if it is to become
> perfect and without deceit. God, now become un-
> utterable, is stripped of all attributes . . . this ascent
> of God from the breathing heart, covering the

whole heavens and descending as rain. But any open avowal of this would be too much...when the abyss between God and ourselves is admitted, — even this abyss is full of the darkness of God, and if ever anyone feels it, let him go down into it and howl there (this is more necessary than crossing over it). Only for him to whom the abyss was a dwelling-place will paradise be retrieved, and every thing deeply and passionately *here*, which the Church has pirated and pawned to a Beyond.[6]

We hold ourselves as we are in his presence. We offer our attention to the darkness. We stand in the humility of our desire. We allow the "distractions" of our fantasy to circle, and we open these also to our mutual scrutiny. "To set about hunting down distractions would be to fall into their trap, when all that is necessary is to turn back to our heart: for distractions reveal to us what we are attached to, and this humble awareness before the Lord should awaken our preferential love for him and lead us to offer him our heart to be purified. Therein lies the battle, the choice of which master to serve."[7]

What does the symbolism of my fantasy life, the obsession with sexual satisfaction, disclose about me at the deepest level of myself? We should not be obsessed by eradication schemes, zero tolerance toward all images; we should allow whatever occurs to remind us of who we are at this moment and create a situation that arouses

our loving energy, identifies decoys, disengages and re-
applies the energy to the one with whom we want to
engage. Such is the dialectic of prayer.

The red thread that tightens into a noose around the
object of desire can be followed back to its origin in the
otherwise inaccessible depths of my own heart. Such intimacy with myself is essential. It is the locus of love. The
combination of our desire with the translucency of humility creates a fluorescence in the darkness. We become
illuminated flarepaths to the ground of our own being,
both for ourselves and for others hoping to land accu-
rately. Desire is the road to being. Our task as lovers is to
maintain that road with care and walk it with precision.

NOTES

1. Blood on the Moon

1. E. M. Forster, *A Passage to India* (Harmondsworth, U.K.: Penguin, 1962), 124.

2. Ibid., 187.

3. Ibid.

2. The Source, the Movement, and the Object of Desire

1. This and the following two extracts are from *The Confessions of St. Augustine*, trans. F. J. Sheed (London: Sheed & Ward, 1944), 49–52.

2. Gustave Flaubert, *Madame Bovary*, trans. Alan Russell (Harmondsworth, U.K.: Penguin Classics, 1959), 295, 301–2.

3. Ibid., 224–25.

4. Denis de Rougemont, *Passion and Society* (London: Faber, 1956), 55.

5. Thomas Mann, *Joseph and His Brothers*, vol. 3: *Joseph in Egypt* (London: Sphere Books, 1968), 362.

6. *Twelfth Night*, II, iv, 15–20.

7. Ibid. II, iv, 113–16.

8. Mann, *Joseph and His Brothers*, 3:344–45.

9. Ibid.

10. Alexander Solzhenitsyn, *The First Circle* (London: Fontana, 1971), 257.

11. My presentation of Lacan's point of view has been refined and enriched by conversations with and corrections made by Diarmuid Rooney. However, he cannot be held responsible for any eventual indictment of these pages for misrepresentation.

3. Pleasure for Pleasure

1. St. Augustine, *De Moribus Ecclesiae Catholicae et de Moribus Manichaeorum* 1, 3, 4: PL 32, 1312.

2. Thomas Aquinas, *De Spe*, a. 3, c. This analysis of love in St. Thomas Aquinas is indebted to Louis-B. Geiger's book *Le problème de l'amour chez saint Thomas d'Aquin*, Paris, 1952.

4. Thirsting for God

1. Andrew Nugent, reviewing the film in the *Irish Press*, July 4, 1977.

2. What I say about the Gospel of St. John is taken from Raymond Brown, *The Death of the Messiah: From Gethsemane to the Grave* (New York: Doubleday, 1994), esp. 2:1070–75.

3. Tertullian, *Apology* 21:19; CC1.126.

4. From William Blake, "The Everlasting Gospel," in *Blake: Poems and Letters*, ed. J. Bronowski (Harmondsworth, U.K.: Penguin, 1986), 75.

5. Joseph Maréchal, "The Problem of 'Mystical Grace in Islam,'" in *Studies in the Psychology of the Mystics* (London: Burns, Oates and Washbourne, 1927). This passage is written after the data, almost all unpublished, supplied by M. Louis Masignon, in *La Passion d'al Hosayn-ibn-Mansour al Hallaj, martyr mystique de l'Islam*, 2 vols. (Paris: Geuthner, 1922).

5. God's Crackpot Love

1. Emily Brontë, *Wuthering Heights and Selected Poems* (London: Pan Books, 1973), 103.

2. Ibid., 348. This poem was written in January 1846, a year before *Wuthering Heights* was published.

3. There are many studies of the Trinity that have been helpful to me in my own understanding of this most important yet ungraspable mystery. The one I find most strikingly articulate and from which I have borrowed here is Catherine Mowry LaCugna, *God for Us: The Trinity and Christian Life* (New York: Harper, 1991).

4. Wilhelm Reich, *Character Analysis* (London: Vision Press, 1973), 345.

5. This etymology was suggested to me by Bernard Lauret when I first saw the film in Paris in 1969.

6. William James, *Varieties of Religious Experience* (London: Longmans, Green, 1904), 212.

7. Ibid., 208.

8. Ibid., 99.

9. "The Pot Geranium" by Norman Nicholson from his book *The Pot Geranium* (London: Faber and Faber, 1954).

6. The Way through the Wandering Rocks

1. Peter Brown, *The Body and Society* (New York: Columbia University Press, 1988), 231.

2. Denis de Rougemont, *Passion and Society* (London: Faber 1956), 320.

3. Brown, *The Body and Society*, 133.

4. From "Casino" by W. H. Auden, in *Collected Shorter Poems, 1927–1957* (London: Faber, 1966), 97.

5. Lillian Feder, *Ancient Myth in Modern Poetry* (Princeton, N.J.: Princeton University Press, 1977), 146.

6. de Rougemont, *Passion and Society*, 145.

7. Example taken from Omraam Mikhael Aivanhov's lecture *The Spiritual Laser* (Prosveta Editions, 1982).

8. These facts are presented in a compelling and accessible way by Brian Swimme and Thomas Berry in *The Universe Story* (London: Penguin, 1992). I have borrowed from p. 260 of this book in these last two paragraphs.

9. I have developed this point and extended the argument in *Kissing the Dark: Connecting with the Unconscious* (Dublin: Veritas, 1999).

10. David Guterson, *Snow Falling on Cedars* (London: Bloomsbury, 1995), 72–73.

11. Laurens Van Der Post, *Venture to the Interior* (Harmondsworth, U.K.: Penguin, 1957), 212.

12. I am paraphrasing Denis Vasse, *Le temps du desir* (Paris: Editions du Seuil, 1972).

13. Brian Friel, *Dancing at Lughnasa* (London: Faber, 1990), 71.

14. See John J. L. Mood, *Rilke on Love and Other Difficulties: Translations and Considerations of Rainer Maria Rilke* (New York: Norton Paperback, 1993), 27–37.

7. Beyond the Pathetic

1. Otto F. Kernberg, M.D., *Love Relations, Normality and Pathology* (New Haven, Conn.: Yale University Press, 1995), 42–45.

2. Martin Heidegger, *Being and Time,* trans. John Macquarrie and Edward Robinson (New York: Harper and Row, 1962), 240.

3. Rainer Maria Rilke, *Poems 1906 to 1926,* trans. J. B. Leishman (London: Hogarth, 1976), 183. This poem was written in Paris on June 20, 1914. The information I give here about Rilke and this poem is taken from Leishman's introduction, 43–44, and from David Kleinbard, *The Beginning of Terror: A Psychological Study of Rainer Maria Rilke's Life and Work* (New York: New York University Press, 1993).

4. Oliver Sacks, "Scotoma: Forgetting and Neglect in Science," in *Hidden Histories of Science,* ed. B. Silvers (London: Granta, 1997), 176–77.

5. R. C. Lewontin, "Genes, Environment, and Organisms," in Silvers, *Hidden Histories,* 136.

6. Thomas Mann, *Joseph and His Brothers,* vol. 4: *Joseph the Provider* (London: Sphere Books, 1968), 202.

7. Pierre Teilhard de Chardin, *The Future of Man* (Harmondsworth, U.K.: London: Penguin, 1971), 245.

8. Ibid., 184.

8. Intimacy with God

1. From *The Spiritual Canticle of St. John of the Cross,* in *The Collected Works of St. John of the Cross,* trans. Kieran Kavanagh and

Otilio Rodriguez (Washington, D.C.: ICS Publications, 1991), 471–77.

2. Evelyn Underhill, *Mysticism* (London: Methuen, 1961).

3. T. S. Eliot, *Four Quartets* (London: Faber, 1944), 44.

4. Commentary on Stanza 39 of The Spiritual Canticle, nos. 3 and 4, in *The Collected Works of St. John of the Cross*, 622–23.

5. Ibid., 567.

6. Rainer Maria Rilke, *Selected Letters, 1902–1926* (London: Quartet Books, 1988), 373–74.

7. *Catechism of the Catholic Church*, Part IV, Christian Prayer (New York: Doubleday, 1995), no. 2729.

Of Related Interest

Ronald Rolheiser
AGAINST AN INFINITE HORIZON
The Finger of God in our Everyday Lives

Full of personal anecdotes, healing wisdom, and a fresh reflection on Scripture, *Against an Infinite Horizon* draws on the
great traditions of parable and storytelling. In this prequel to
the bestselling *The Holy Longing,* Rolheiser's new fans will be
delighted with further insights into social justice, sexuality,
mortality, the benefits of community, and rediscovering the
deep beauty and poetry of Christian spirituality.

Do you ever feel that your meditation is just a small corner
of the divine in a difficult world? Ronald Rolheiser invites us
to see meditation, and every aspect of life, as part of a world
filled with God and brimming with possibility and hope.

"Ronald Rolheiser has mastered the old, old art of parable."
— Morris West

"A felicitous blend of scriptural reflection, shrewd psychological observations, and generous portions of letters sent to
Rolheiser and his responses."   — *Commonweal*

0-8245-1965-5, $16.95 paperback

crossroad

Of Related Interest

Fran Ferder and John Heagle
TENDER FIRES
The Spiritual Promise of Sexuality

"Here is a book as generous in its wisdom as it is exact in its observation of the human struggle to make the many voices of sexuality sing in harmony."
— Eugene Kennedy, author of *The Unhealed Wound*

Who has not struggled with sexuality and religion? For decades, Sr. Fran Ferder, F.S.P.A, Ph.D., and Fr. John Heagle, M.A., J.C.L, have been listening to the stories of people's joys, sorrows, and dilemmas, as well as their efforts to integrate sexuality, faith, and church membership. In *Tender Fires*, Ferder and Heagle delicately reveal how the power of the erotic extends not just to sex but to every corner of existence.

0-8245-1982-5, $16.95 paperback

Please support your local bookstore,
or call 1-800-707-0670 for Customer Service.

For a free catalog, write us at

THE CROSSROAD PUBLISHING COMPANY
16 Penn Plaza, 481 Eighth Avenue
New York, NY 10001

Visit our website at
www.crossroadpublishing.com
All prices subject to change.

crossroad